COMPARATIVE STATICS ANALYSIS in ECONOMICS

COMPARATIVE
STATICS
ANALYSIS in
ECONOMICS

Kevin M. Currier

Department of Economics
Oklahoma State University

World Scientific
Singapore • New Jersey • London • Hong Kong

Published by

World Scientific Publishing Co. Pte. Ltd.

5 Toh Tuck Link, Singapore 596224

USA office: 27 Warren Street, Suite 401-402, Hackensack, NJ 07601

UK office: 57 Shelton Street, Covent Garden, London WC2H 9HE

British Library Cataloguing-in-Publication Data
A catalogue record for this book is available from the British Library.

COMPARATIVE STATICS ANALYSIS IN ECONOMICS

ISBN-13 978-981-02-4366-1
ISBN-10 981-02-4366-9

To my parents

Preface

As an empirical science, economics employs theoretical models to describe economic phenomena and processes. These models are then used to generate empirically testable hypotheses. Comparative statics analysis facilitates the derivation of such hypotheses. This book is a self-contained introduction to comparative statics analysis.

The demands that modern economic analysis places upon the student renders an incremental approach to learning essential. This permits students' intuition to develop as mathematical tools are employed in problem solving. In this book, students learn comparative statics analysis by doing comparative statics in progressively more sophisticated models. Repeated application of the basic technique allows students to gain competence in comparative statics analysis with minimal distractions.

Comparative Statics Analysis in Economics presupposes knowledge of intermediate microeconomic theory and the ability on the part of the student to compute the partial derivatives of a function of several variables. While the level of mathematical sophistication has been kept as elementary as possible, understanding of some additional preliminary results is essential. These preliminaries are summarized in Chapter 1.

Chapter 2 is devoted to a discussion of the comparative statics methodology. Simple examples provide the motivation for the remainder of the text. The Implicit Function Theorem is presented, and we discuss the basic comparative statics technique.

In Chapter 3, we examine the comparative statics properties of models with explicit solutions. These are the simplest type of comparative statics problems and serve to illustrate concretely the dependence of the "solution" values of a model on its parameters.

In Chapter 4, we pass to a discussion of general function models. Having clearly illustrated the dependence of solutions on parameters in Chapter 3, the transition to models with arbitrary functional forms satisfying a minimal set of assumptions is relatively straightforward. The presentation here is intentionally repetitious in order to emphasize the common structure of the models, the applicability of the Implicit Function Theorem, and the importance of the second-order sufficient conditions in optimization-based models. Moreover, it is in this chapter that the ability of the comparative statics methodology to generate qualitative results becomes most evident.

Chapter 5 presents the basic comparative statics theorems for parameterized optimization problems. In order to reinforce the technique, the theorems are proven using the formal methodology of Chapter 4.

Chapter 6 provides an introduction to primal-dual analysis. The ability of this method to yield all implications of the optimization hypothesis is emphasized, while formal proofs of some claims are omitted.

No results have been presented without application. In addition, the exercises at the ends of the chapters involve application of the techniques and results presented in the chapters. These exercises should be considered an *essential* part of the text, as one masters the technique only through its application. Answers to selected problems are presented in the back of the book.

Contents

Acknowledgments

This book reflects the experience of Ph.D. students at Oklahoma State University, and I wish to thank them for the stimulus they have provided. I would like to express my gratitude to Kwan Yun and Michael Jerison for introducing me to these fascinating topics. A special thanks to Susanne Rassouli-Atkinson and Keith Willett for their assistance and support in this project. I wish also to express my deepest gratitude to David Sharp and Kim Tan, my editors at World Scientific Publishing Co. Without their efforts, this project would not have been initiated, let alone completed. Finally, I am indebted to my typist, Bev Dunham, for her patience and skill in the preparation of the text. All remaining errors are my responsibility.

Kevin M. Currier

1. Mathematical Preliminaries

For convenience, the mathematical concepts and results needed to study comparative statics are summarized in this chapter. This is not intended as a comprehen-
sive treatment of these topics. It serves only as a concise summary and convenient
reference.

1.1 Differentiable Functions

If the function $y = f(x_1, \ldots, x_n)$ has continuous first-order partial derivatives
everywhere in its domain, we say f is C^1. If all partial derivatives up to and
including order K exist and are themselves continuous functions, we say f is C^K.

Example 1.1

For the case of $n = 1$, consider the function $y = f(x) = x^{8/3}$. This function is a C^2
function since $f'''(x)$ is undefined at $x = 0$.

1.2 The Chain Rule

Suppose that $y = f(x_1, \ldots, x_n)$ is a C^1 function. Furthermore, suppose that the x's
are themselves C^1 functions of the variables a and b, i.e.,

$x_1 = x_1\,(a,\,b),\,.\,.\,.,\,x_n = x_n\,(a,\,b).$

Then $\dfrac{\partial y}{\partial a} = f_1\dfrac{\partial x_1}{\partial a} + \,.\,.\,.\, + f_n\dfrac{\partial x_n}{\partial a}$

and $\dfrac{\partial y}{\partial b} = f_1\dfrac{\partial x_1}{\partial b} + \,.\,.\,.\, + f_n\dfrac{\partial x_n}{\partial b}$

where $f_i = \partial f/\partial x_i$, $i = 1,\,.\,.\,.,\,n.$

Example 1.2

Suppose $y = f\,(x_1,\,x_2) = x_1^2 + x_1x_2$ where $x_1 = a^2$ and $x_2 = a + b$. Then using the Chain Rule, we obtain

$$\begin{aligned}
\frac{\partial y}{\partial a} &= \left(2x_1 + x_2\right)(2a) + x_1(1) \\
&= \left(2a^2 + a + b\right)(2a) + a^2 \\
&= 4a^3 + 3a^2 + 2ab
\end{aligned}$$

and $\dfrac{\partial y}{\partial b} = \left(2x_1 + x_2\right)(0) + x_1\,(1) = a^2.$

Note that if we substitute $x_1 = a^2$ and $x_2 = a + b$ directly into $x_1^2 + x_1x_2$ we obtain $y = a^4 + a^3 + a^2b.$

Computing $\partial y/\partial a$ and $\partial y/\partial b$ directly yields $\dfrac{\partial y}{\partial a} = 4a^3 + 3a^2 + 2ab$ and $\dfrac{\partial y}{\partial b} = a^2,$ which are precisely the results obtained using the Chain Rule.

1.3 Determinants

The *determinant* of the 2×2 matrix

$$A = \begin{vmatrix} a_{11} & a_{12} \\ a_{21} & a_{22} \end{vmatrix}$$

denoted by $|A|$ is, $|A| = a_{11}\,a_{22} - a_{12}\,a_{21}$. The determinant of the 3×3 matrix

$$A = \begin{vmatrix} a_{11} & a_{12} & a_{13} \\ a_{21} & a_{22} & a_{23} \\ a_{31} & a_{32} & a_{33} \end{vmatrix}$$

is

$$a_{11} \begin{vmatrix} a_{22} & a_{23} \\ a_{32} & a_{33} \end{vmatrix} - a_{21} \begin{vmatrix} a_{12} & a_{13} \\ a_{32} & a_{33} \end{vmatrix} + a_{31} \begin{vmatrix} a_{12} & a_{13} \\ a_{22} & a_{23} \end{vmatrix}.$$

1.4 Cramer's Rule

Consider the system of equations

$$a_{11}\,x_1 + a_{12}\,x_2 + a_{13}\,x_3 = b_1$$

$$a_{21}\,x_1 + a_{22}\,x_2 + a_{23}\,x_3 = b_2$$

$$a_{31}\,x_1 + a_{32}\,x_2 + a_{33}\,x_3 = b_3.$$

When $|A| = \begin{vmatrix} a_{11} & a_{12} & a_{13} \\ a_{21} & a_{22} & a_{23} \\ a_{31} & a_{32} & a_{33} \end{vmatrix} \neq 0,$ the unique solution to this three-equation

system is:

$$x_1 = \frac{\begin{vmatrix} b_1 & a_{12} & a_{13} \\ b_2 & a_{22} & a_{23} \\ b_3 & a_{32} & a_{33} \end{vmatrix}}{|A|}, x_2 = \frac{\begin{vmatrix} a_{11} & b_1 & a_{13} \\ a_{21} & b_2 & a_{23} \\ a_{31} & b_3 & a_{33} \end{vmatrix}}{|A|}, x_3 = \frac{\begin{vmatrix} a_{11} & a_{12} & b_1 \\ a_{21} & a_{22} & b_2 \\ a_{31} & a_{32} & b_3 \end{vmatrix}}{|A|}.$$

1.5 Optimization, $f: R \rightarrow R$

Consider the following graph of the function $y = f(x)$:

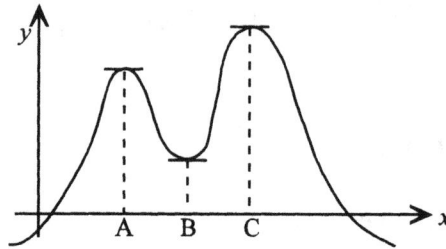

Figure 1.1

Suppose f is C^2. (We shall limit our discussions to consideration of maxima and minima that occur within the interior of the domain of f.) Points A, B, C, are *local extrema*. Points A and C are *local maxima*; point B is a *local minimum*. Note that the slope of the tangent line is zero at each of these points. A *necessary condition* for f to have a local maximum or minimum is $f'(x) = 0$. Any point where $f'(x) = 0$ is called a *critical point*. If, at a critical point x^*, $f''(x^*) < 0$, then x^* is a local maximum. If at a critical point x^*, $f''(x^*) > 0$, then x^* is a local minimum. Note that these are *sufficient conditions*.

1.6 Optimization, $f\colon R^2 \to R$

Suppose $y = f(x_1, x_2)$ is a C^2 function. A necessary condition for a local maximum or minimum at $\left(x_1^*, x_2^*\right)$ is

$$\frac{\partial f}{\partial x_1} = f_1 = 0, \quad \frac{\partial f}{\partial x_2} = f_2 = 0$$

at this point. This implies that the *tangent plane* at $\left(x_1^*, x_2^*, y^*\right)$ is horizontal. As before, any point where $f_1 = f_2 = 0$ is a critical point. To distinguish local maxima from local minima, form the *Hessian matrix* of second-order partial derivatives

$$H = \begin{bmatrix} f_{11} & f_{12} \\ f_{21} & f_{22} \end{bmatrix}.$$

If, at a critical point, $f_{11} < 0$ and $|H| > 0$, then this critical point is a local maximum, in which case we say that the Hessian matrix is *negative definite*. If, at a critical point, $f_{11} > 0$ and $|H| > 0$, then this critical point is a local minimum and the Hessian matrix is *positive definite*. These are the higher dimensional analogs of the single variable results discussed in Section 1.5. A local maximum and a local minimum of a function of two variables are depicted in Figures 1.2 and 1.3.

Tangent Plane

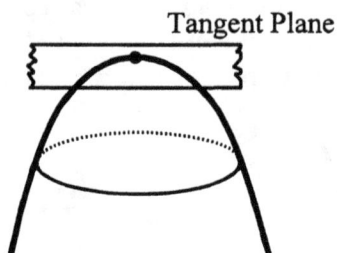

Figure 1.2

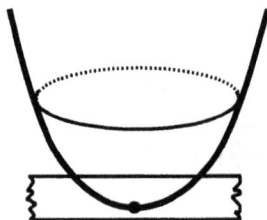

Figure 1.3

Example 1.3.

Consider the function

$$y = f(x_1, x_2) = 10x_1 + 12x_2 - x_1^2 - 6x_2^2.$$

We find the critical point(s) by solving

$$f_1 = 10 - 2x_1 = 0, \quad f_2 = 12 - 12x_2 = 0$$

implying that the unique critical point of f is at $x_1 = 5$, $x_2 = 1$. Noting that

$$H = \begin{bmatrix} -2 & 0 \\ 0 & -12 \end{bmatrix}$$

with $-2 = f_{11} < 0$ and $|H| = 24 > 0$ establishes the point $(5, 1)$ as a maximum of f. At $(5, 1)$ the graph of this function looks like Figure 1.2.

1.7 Constrained Optimization, Two Variables, One Constraint

Consider the problem of finding the extrema of $f(x_1, x_2)$ subject to $g(x_1, x_2) = 0$ where f and g are C^2. The function f is called the *objective function* and g is called the *constraint*. We are in search of the maxima and minima of f, given that our search must be restricted to the set of points satisfying the equation $g(x_1, x_2) = 0$. To solve the problem, form the *Lagrangian* function

$$L(x_1, x_2, \lambda) = f(x_1, x_2) + \lambda g(x_1, x_2).$$

The variable λ is called the *Lagrange multiplier*. The first-order necessary conditions for a maximum or minimum are

$$L_1 = f_1 + \lambda g_1 = 0$$

$$L_2 = f_2 + \lambda g_2 = 0 \tag{1}$$

$$L_\lambda = g(x_1, x_2) = 0.$$

To distinguish maxima from minima, form the *Bordered Hessian* matrix

$$H = \begin{bmatrix} L_{11} & L_{12} & g_1 \\ L_{21} & L_{22} & g_2 \\ g_1 & g_2 & 0 \end{bmatrix}.$$

At any point where (1) holds, if $|H| > 0$, then f has a maximum subject to $g(x_1, x_2) = 0$. If, at any point where (1) holds, $|H| < 0$, f has a minimum subject to $g(x_1, x_2) = 0$. Again, these are sufficient conditions.

Example 1.4

Consider

Maximize $\quad x_1^2 x_2$
x_1, x_2

subject to $x_1 + 2x_2 - 6 = 0$.

Writing

$$L\left(x_1, x_2, \lambda\right) = x_1^2 x_2 + \lambda\left(x_1 + 2x_2 - 6\right)$$

the first-order necessary conditions for a maximum are

$$L_1 = 2x_1 x_2 + \lambda = 0$$

$$L_2 = x_1^2 + 2\lambda = 0$$

$$L_\lambda = x_1 + 2x_2 - 6 = 0.$$

Solving, one obtains $x_1 = 4$, $x_2 = 1$, $\lambda = -8$. Form the Bordered Hessian

$$H = \begin{bmatrix} 2x_2 & 2x_1 & 1 \\ 2x_1 & 0 & 2 \\ 1 & 2 & 0 \end{bmatrix}$$

which, when evaluated at $x_1 = 4$, $x_2 = 1$ yields

$$H = \begin{bmatrix} 2 & 8 & 1 \\ 8 & 0 & 2 \\ 1 & 2 & 0 \end{bmatrix}$$

with $|H| > 0$, implying $(4, 1)$ is a constrained maximum of $x_1^2 x_2$. In solving this problem, we found the point on the line $x_1 + 2x_2 = 6$ where the value of $x_1^2 x_2$ is largest.

2. The Methodology of Comparative Statics

In economic modeling, we make a distinction between variables whose values are determined within (or by) the model and variables whose values enter the model as constants determined outside the model. Variables whose values are determined within the model are referred to as *endogenous variables*, and variables whose values are determined outside the model are referred to as *exogenous variables*. For example, consider a profit maximizing firm producing an output from a single input, labor. The firm's output level is *chosen* by the firm so as to maximize profit, whereas the wage rate that the firm pays its workers may be determined by market forces *beyond the control* of the firm. Hence we say that the firm's output level is an endogenous variable and that the wage rate is an exogenous variable. Or, in the model of consumer behavior, the consumer chooses consumption levels (endogenous variables) but takes the prices of the goods as exogenously given constants (exogenous variables). We shall adopt the common convention of referring to endogenous variables simply as *variables* and exogenous variables as *parameters*.

Comparative Statics is the formal study of how the equilibrium or optimal values of the variables in a model are affected by changes in the values of the parameters in the model.

Example 2.1

Consider a supply and demand model of the market for some commodity x with price p. The market is illustrated in Figure 2.1 where p^* and x^* denote the equilibrium price and quantity in the market.

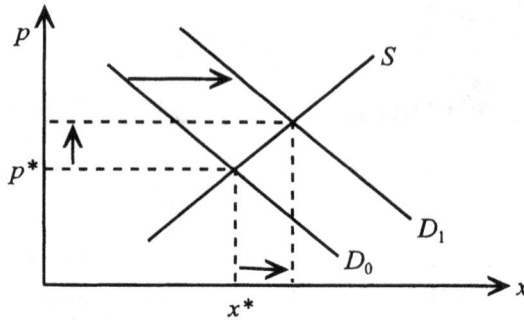

Figure 2.1

Along a given demand curve, consumer income is held constant. If income changes, the demand curve will typically shift to the right or the left. Suppose the good is a *normal good* so that an increase in consumer income will shift the demand curve for x to the right. The effect of the income increase is shown in Figure 2.1 as the rightward shift in the demand curve from D_0 to D_1. The change in the parameter (income) has caused an increase in the equilibrium values of the variables (price and quantity). Asserting that when income increases, $p*$ and $x*$ also increase is a simple example of *equilibrium comparative statics*.

Example 2.2

Consider now a profit maximizing monopoly producing output y from labor input x where the exogenously given wage rate that the firm must pay its workers is w. The demand curve (D) for the firm's output, the corresponding marginal revenue (MR) curve as well as the firm's marginal cost (MC) curve are shown in Figure 2.2.

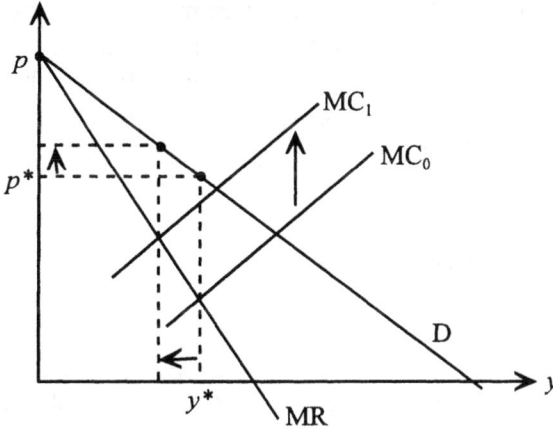

Figure 2.2

The monopoly maximizes profit by producing the output level y^*, where MR = MC. The output is sold at price p^*. Now typically the firm's marginal cost curve will depend on the value of w. An increase in w will generally shift the MC curve upward, as illustrated in Figure 2.2. This change causes the monopolist to decrease y^* and increase p^*. Asserting that an increase in the wage rate (the parameter) will decrease the monopoly output level and increase price (the variables) is an example of *comparative statics with optimization*.

2.1. Comparative Statics and Empirical Testing

Comparative statics analysis is valuable in that it provides a means for generating *testable hypotheses*. For example, consider the monopolist discussed in Example 2.2. It can never be directly proven that a firm maximizes profit. However, if the monopolist is maximizing profit, our model predicts that an increase in w will systematically lead to a higher selling price p^* and a lower output level y^*. If we then look at the behavior of an actual monopoly and we observe that in the presence of a wage increase, p^* rises and y^* falls, we have empirical evidence of the validity of the hypothesis that the monopolist maximizes profit. Our model has allowed us to assert that if the firm *does* maximize profit, certain economic behavior should be observed in the presence of the wage increase. If that behavior does actually occur, we have provided evidence that the hypothesis of profit maximization is valid. The evidence then *supports* the theory, though the theory is not (and can never be) proved.

2.2. Implicit Differentiation

The graphical technique employed in the first section is of limited value because we are restricted to two dimensional analysis, whereas many economic applications involve more than two variables. In addition, the graphical technique allows us to make assertions regarding the *direction* of change but says nothing about the *magnitude* of the induced changes in the variables. Comparative statics therefore employs the methods of single and multivariable calculus.

Our main tool will be the method of *implicit differentiation*. Suppose a relation between x and y is expressed by an equation such as

$$x^2 + 2xy + y^5 - 3 = 0. \tag{1}$$

It may be difficult or impossible to solve this equation explicitly for y in terms of x. Or, the solution may not even express y as a function of x. However, in general it *will* be possible to determine an explicit expression for dy/dx. To this end, *suppose* there is some function $y = f(x)$ that satisfies (1). Substituting into (1) yields

$$x^2 + 2xf(x) + \left[f(x)\right]^5 - 3 = 0. \tag{2}$$

Differentiating (2) using the product rule and the chain rule yields

$$2x + 2xf'(x) + 2f(x) + 5\left[f(x)\right]^4 f'(x) = 0.$$

Solving for $f'(x)$ we obtain

$$f'(x) = \frac{-2x - 2f(x)}{2x + 5[f(x)]^4}.$$

Now, recalling that $f(x) = y$, we have

$$f'(x) = \frac{dy}{dx} = \frac{-2x - 2y}{2x + 5y^4}. \tag{3}$$

We may now use (3) to compute the slope of the curve given by (1) at any (x, y) pair satisfying (1). For example, the curve passes through the point $(1, 1)$ and (3) tells us that the slope of the curve at this point is $(-2 - 2)/(2 + 5) = -4/7$. We have succeeded in computing the *slope* of the curve at the point $(1, 1)$ even though we do not have an explicit representation of the function itself. The precise conditions under which this is possible will be discussed in Section 2.3. It is instructive to convince oneself that the method works by employing some simple examples such as $6x^2 - 2y = 0$ and $y^2 - 4x = 0$ where we can solve for y explicitly in terms of x and computing dy/dx in the usual way as well as via the implicit technique.

2.3. The Implicit Function Theorem (One Variable, One Parameter)

In general, we will be interested in solving various economic relationships for the variables in terms of the parameters; so as a first step, suppose we have a relation between a variable x and a parameter a given by $F(x, a) = 0$. This defines a curve in (x, a) space in the same way that Equation (1) in Section 2.2 defined a curve in (x, y) space. Now, suppose we are interested in the behavior of this relationship at some particular point (x_0, a_0) satisfying $F(x_0, a_0) = 0$. Suppose further that near this point, the curve can be described by a function $x = x(a)$ (even though we may not be able to explicitly write it down). Then, since $x = x(a)$ near (x_0, a_0), the relation $F(x, a) = 0$ becomes an *identity* when we substitute $x = x(a)$ into it; i.e.,

$F(x(a), a) \equiv 0$ for all a near a_0. Now, differentiation of equalities is not valid, but differentiation of identities is valid. Since $F(x(a), a) \equiv 0$ for all a near a_0 is an identity, we may differentiate both sides with respect to a, obtaining

$$F_x\big(x(a), a\big)x'(a) + F_a\big(x(a), a\big) = 0.$$

Therefore

$$x'(a) = \frac{-F_a\big(x(a), a\big)}{F_x\big(x(a), a\big)}. \tag{4}$$

Since $x_0 = x(a_0)$, this formula implies that the slope of the curve at the point (x_0, a_0) is

$$x'(a_0) = \frac{-F_a\big(x_0, a_0\big)}{F_x\big(x_0, a_0\big)}.$$

Note that this formula is meaningful as long as $F_x(x_0, a_0) \neq 0$.

Return for a moment to the distinction between equalities and identities referred to above. A relation like $2x = 7$ is an *equality* and is true "sometimes," i.e., only when $x = 3.5$. A relation such as $x^2 = x \cdot x$ is an *identity* and is true "always," i.e., for all x. Differentiation of an equality is not valid, as can be seen from differentiation of the expression $2x = 7$, which yields $2 = 0$. Differentiation of an identity is valid, however, as can be seen by differentiating $x^2 = x \cdot x$ using the product rule, obtaining $2x = x(1) + x(1)$.

The preceding discussion is summarized by the following.

Implicit Function Theorem (One Variable, One Parameter)

Let $F(x, a)$ be a C^1 function and consider the point (x_0, a_0) satisfying the relation $F(x_0, a_0) = 0$. If $F_x(x_0, a_0) \neq 0$, then there is a C^1 function $x = x(a)$ defined near a_0 such that

(i) $F\big(x(a), a\big) \equiv 0$ for all a near a_0,

(ii) $x(a_0) = x_0$, and

(iii) $x'(a_0) = -\dfrac{F_a\!\left(x_0, a_0\right)}{F_x\!\left(x_0, a_0\right)}.$

Figure 2.3 provides an illustration.

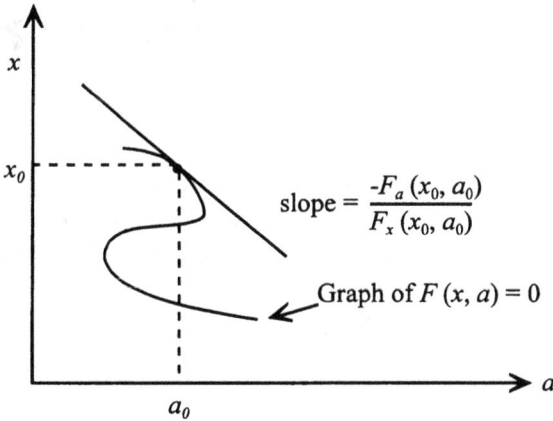

Figure 2.3

The Implicit Function Theorem tells us that as long as $F_x(x_0, a_0) \neq 0$, we can, in principle, solve for x in terms of a and obtain the slope of the curve via the formula given by (iii).

Example 2.3

Consider the equation $F(x, a) = 2x - a^2 = 0$ at the point $(x_0, a_0) = (2, 2)$. Since $F_x = 2 \neq 0$, the hypothesis of the Implicit Function Theorem is satisfied and the slope of this curve in (x, a) space is given by $-F_a / F_x = -(-2a)/2 = a$. Therefore, at $(x_0, a_0) = (2, 2)$, the slope is 2. An illustration is provided in Figure 2.4.

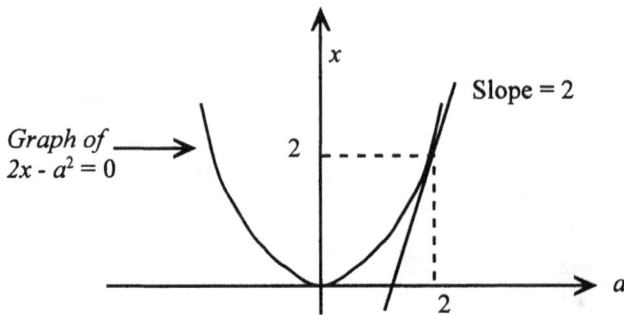

Figure 2.4

Observe that in this particular example, an explicit differentiable function may be found that can be seen to satisfy (i) – (iii): Since $2x - a^2 = 0$, we have $x(a) = a^2 / 2$ so $x'(a) = a$. Note also that when the function $x(a) = a^2 / 2$ is substituted back into the equation $2x - a^2 = 0$, it is transformed into an identity since $2x(a) - a^2 = 2 (a^2 / 2) - a^2 \equiv 0$. This is precisely why (i) – (iii) are valid.

Example 2.4

Consider the equation $F(x, a) = a^2x^3 + ax - 2 = 0$ at the point $(1, 1)$. As before, this relation defines a curve in (x, a) space. We cannot, however, solve explicitly for x in terms of a as we did in Example 2.3. Observe that $F_x = 3a^2x^2 + a$ so $F_x (1, 1) = 4 \neq 0$, and the Implicit Function Theorem tells us that the equation $a^2x^3 + ax - 2 = 0$ does actually define x as a differentiable function of a near $a = 1$ and that its slope is

$$x'(a) = \frac{-F_a(x, a)}{F_x(x, a)} = \frac{-2ax^3 - x}{3a^2x^2 + a},$$

which, when evaluated at $(1, 1)$ is $-\frac{3}{4}$.

If we had simply assumed that there is a function $x = x(a)$ satisfying

$$a^2 [x(a)]^3 + a[x(a)] - 2 = 0$$

implicit differentiation yields

$$a^2 \left(3[x(a)]^2 x'(a) \right) + [x(a)]^3 (2a) + ax'(a) + x(a) = 0,$$

which when solved for $x'(a)$ yields

$$x'(a) = \frac{-2ax^3 - x}{3a^2 x^2 + a},$$

which is precisely what we obtained using the formula

$$x'(a) = -F_a(x, a)/F_x(x, a).$$

2.4 The Implicit Function Theorem (Two Variables, One Parameter)

In many of our applications, we will encounter systems of relations between variables and parameters such as

$$F^1(x, y, a) = x^2 - ay = 0$$

$$F^2(x, y, a) = xy - a = 0. \tag{5}$$

Suppose we are interested in these relationships at the point $(x_0, y_0, a_0) = (1, 1, 1)$, which does indeed satisfy (5). Assuming that x and y can be expressed as differentiable functions of a, write $x = x(a)$, $y = y(a)$ and substitute into (5):

$$[x(a)]^2 - ay(a) \equiv 0$$

$$x(a)\, y(a) - a \equiv 0.$$

Differentiating each identity with respect to a yields

$2x(a)\, x'(a) - ay'(a) - y(a) = 0$

$x(a)\, y'(a) + y(a)\, x'(a) - 1 = 0.$

Solving for $x'(a)$ and $y'(a)$ yields

$$x'(a) = \frac{xy + a}{2x^2 + ay}$$

$$y'(a) = \frac{2x - y^2}{2x^2 + ay}.$$

(6)

Evaluating these at the point $(1, 1, 1)$ we obtain $x'(1) = \frac{2}{3}$ and $y'(1) = \frac{1}{3}$.

Observe now that if we compute the *Jacobian matrix* J of partial derivatives

$$J = \begin{bmatrix} F_x^1 & F_y^1 \\ F_x^2 & F_y^2 \end{bmatrix} = \begin{bmatrix} 2x & -a \\ y & x \end{bmatrix}$$

the determinant of J is $|J| = 2x^2 + ay$, which is the denominator of the derivatives given in (6). In general, for a system of equations such as (5), as long as $|J| \neq 0$ at any point (x_0, y_0, a_0) satisfying the equations, the functions $x(a)$ and $y(a)$ exist, are differentiable, and the derivatives may be obtained simply by differentiating implicitly as we did above.

This is a three-dimensional analog of the results discussed in Section 2.3, with $|J|$ playing the role that F_x played. For a thorough discussion of the Implicit Function Theorem, see Bartle (1976).

Example 2.5

Consider the system of linear equations

$F^1 (x, y, a) = x + y - 2 = 0$

$$F^2 (x, y, a) = -x + y - a = 0. \tag{7}$$

In this case, explicit solutions may be obtained by solving for x and y in terms of a yielding $x(a) = (2 - a)/2$ and $y(a) = (2 + a)/2$. Differentiating, we obtain $x'(a) = -\frac{1}{2}$ and $y'(a) = \frac{1}{2}$. Using implicit differentiation, write $x = x(a)$, $y = y(a)$, and substitute into (7), obtaining the identities

$$x(a) + y(a) - 2 \equiv 0$$

$$- x(a) + y(a) - a \equiv 0.$$

Differentiating, we obtain

$$x'(a) + y'(a) = 0$$

$$-x'(a) + y'(a) - 1 = 0,$$

implying $x'(a) = -\frac{1}{2}$ and $y'(a) = \frac{1}{2}$. Note that

$$|J| = \begin{vmatrix} F_x^1 & F_y^1 \\ F_x^2 & F_y^2 \end{vmatrix} = \begin{vmatrix} 1 & 1 \\ -1 & 1 \end{vmatrix} \neq 0,$$

validating the assertion of the existence of the differentiable functions $x = x(a)$, $y = y(a)$. Here, the fact that $|J| \neq 0$ reflects the fact that the lines given by (7) are not parallel and hence intersect at a unique point that depends on the value of a. Figure 2.5 provides an illustration.

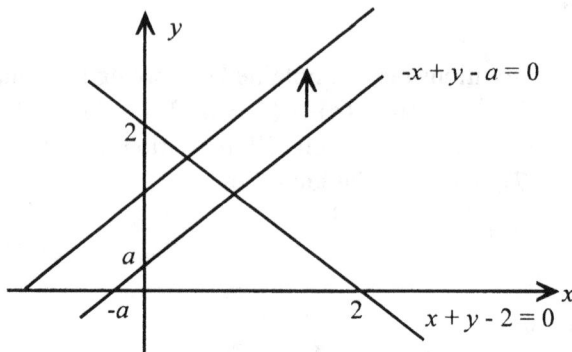

Figure 2.5

In Figure 2.5, we have assumed $a > 0$. The point where the lines intersect depends on the value of a as we saw when we obtained $x(a) = (2 - a)/2$ and $y(a) = (2 + a)/2$. As a changes, the point of intersection changes according to these formulas. The diagram illustrates the effect of an increase in a. Our computations yielded $x'(a) = -\frac{1}{2} < 0$ and $y'(a) = \frac{1}{2} > 0$, which tells us that as a increases, the solution value of x goes down and the solution value of y goes up, as can be seen in the diagram.

2.5. Summary of the Technique of Comparative Statics

For simplicity, we shall restrict our attention to systems involving no more than three equations. The technique is valid, however, for any number of equations, provided that the number of variables equals the number of equations.

Consider first a model involving one variable x and a single parameter a, which is summarized by

$$F(x, a) = 0 \qquad (8)$$

where F is C^1. As long as $F_x \neq 0$, (8) can be solved (in principle) for x as a C^1 function of a:

$x = x^*(a).$

(We will denote these functions with an asterisk * since they will typically denote *equilibrium* or *optimal* values of the variables in our models.)

The comparative statics derivative is obtained by substituting $x = x^*(a)$ into (8), yielding the *identity*

$$F\left(x^*(a),\ a\right) \equiv 0,$$

which, when differentiated, implies

$$\frac{dx^*}{da} = -\frac{F_a}{F_x}.$$

This derivative tells us how the variable x responds to changes in the parameter a, given that the equation $F(x, a) = 0$ must be satisfied.

Now, consider the two variable, two equation, one parameter model summarized by

$$F^1(x, y, a) = 0$$

$$F^2(x, y, a) = 0$$

(9)

where F^1 and F^2 are C^1 functions. Compute the Jacobian determinant

$$|J| = \begin{vmatrix} F_x^1 & F_y^1 \\ F_x^2 & F_y^2 \end{vmatrix}.$$

As long as $|J| \neq 0$, (9) may be solved for the variables as functions of the parameter a:

$$x = x^*(a), \quad y = y^*(a).$$

These functions are C^1, and we obtain their derivatives by substituting them into (9) and differentiating the *identities*

$$F^1\big(x^*(a),\ y^*(a),\ a\big) \equiv 0$$

$$F^2\big(x^*(a),\ y^*(a),\ a\big) \equiv 0,$$

yielding

$$F^1_x\left(\frac{dx^*}{da}\right) + F^1_y\left(\frac{dy^*}{da}\right) + F^1_a = 0$$

$$F^2_x\left(\frac{dx^*}{da}\right) + F^2_y\left(\frac{dy^*}{da}\right) + F^2_a = 0.$$

Using Cramer's Rule to solve for the comparative statics derivatives, we obtain

$$\frac{dx^*}{da} = \frac{\begin{vmatrix} -F^1_a & F^1_y \\ -F^2_a & F^2_y \end{vmatrix}}{\begin{vmatrix} F^1_x & F^1_y \\ F^2_x & F^2_y \end{vmatrix}} = \frac{F^1_y F^2_a - F^1_a F^2_y}{F^1_x F^2_y - F^1_y F^2_x}$$

and

$$\frac{dy^*}{da} = \frac{\begin{vmatrix} F^1_x & -F^1_a \\ F^2_x & -F^2_a \end{vmatrix}}{\begin{vmatrix} F^1_x & F^1_y \\ F^2_x & F^2_y \end{vmatrix}} = \frac{F^1_a F^2_x - F^1_x F^2_a}{F^1_x F^2_y - F^1_y F^2_x}\ .$$

The derivatives dx^*/da and dy^*/da tell us how the variables x and y respond to changes in the value of the parameter a, given that (9) must be satisfied.

Finally, consider the three variable, three equation, one parameter model summarized by

$F^1(x, y, z, a) = 0$

$F^2(x, y, z, a) = 0$ (10)

$F^3(x, y, z, a) = 0$

where F^1, F^2, and F^3 are C^1 functions. Compute the Jacobian determinant

$$|J| = \begin{vmatrix} F_x^1 & F_y^1 & F_z^1 \\ F_x^2 & F_y^2 & F_z^2 \\ F_x^3 & F_y^3 & F_z^3 \end{vmatrix}.$$

Provided that $|J| \neq 0$, we may solve (10) for the variables as functions of the parameter a:

$x = x*(a), y = y*(a), z = z*(a).$

These functions are C^1, and we obtain the comparative statics derivatives dx^*/da, dy^*/da, and dz^*/da by substituting them into (10) and differentiating the *identities*

$F^1\left(x^*(a), y^*(a), z^*(a), a\right) \equiv 0$

$F^2\left(x^*(a), y^*(a), z^*(a), a\right) \equiv 0$

$F^3\left(x^*(a), y^*(a), z^*(a), a\right) \equiv 0$

yielding

$$F_x^1\left(\frac{dx^*}{da}\right) + F_y^1\left(\frac{dy^*}{da}\right) + F_z^1\left(\frac{dz^*}{da}\right) + F_a^1 = 0$$

$$F_x^2\left(\frac{dx^*}{da}\right) + F_y^2\left(\frac{dy^*}{da}\right) + F_z^2\left(\frac{dz^*}{da}\right) + F_a^2 = 0$$

$$F_x^3\left(\frac{dx^*}{da}\right) + F_y^3\left(\frac{dy^*}{da}\right) + F_z^3\left(\frac{dz^*}{da}\right) + F_a^3 = 0$$

and solving for dx^*/da, dy^*/da, and dz^*/da using Cramer's Rule. (Note that if the functions depend on more than one parameter, we obtain the comparative statics derivatives with respect to any parameter by differentiating the appropriate identities with respect to that parameter.)

All comparative statics problems involve the application of this technique to some degree. In some cases, we will have explicit functional forms with which to work. In many instances, however, we have only some general information regarding the properties of the functions. The exact form and content of the functions will depend on the particular application. As we shall see, the requirement that $|J| \neq 0$ will typically be insured by the economic assumptions of the model.

Note: The methodology of comparative statics was fully developed and formalized by Samuelson (1947).

3. Comparative Statics with Explicit Solutions

3.1 Two Classes of Comparative Statics Problems

All comparative statics problems involve the study of the manner in which the solution values of the variables in a system of equations respond to changes in the values of the parameters in the system. In general, these systems of equations will arise in one of two ways. In many economic models, it is assumed that some economic agent is maximizing or minimizing an objective function, perhaps in the presence of one or more constraints. In this class of models, the first-order necessary and the second-order sufficient conditions for a maximum or a minimum define and characterize the choices that will be made by the agent. Comparative statics analysis performed in such a context is called *comparative statics with optimization.*

In other economic models, however, no explicit optimizing behavior is assumed. Examples include supply and demand models, Leontieff input-output models, and the IS-LM macroeconomic model. In this class of models, a system of equations defines an equilibrium position of the model. Comparative statics analysis performed in this context is called *equilibrium comparative statics.*

We begin our study of comparative statics by restricting our attention to a series of applications in which we obtain *explicit solutions.* In these models, specific functional forms with one or more arbitrary parameter values are assumed. The comparative statics derivatives are readily obtained through ordinary differentiation. In Chapter 4, we pass to a more general and useful form of comparative statics analysis in which the assumption of specific functional forms is dispensed with, assuming instead only general functional forms satisfying some minimal set of economic assumptions. In these *general function models*, the implicit techniques discussed in Chapter 2 will be most useful.

3.2 Equilibrium Comparative Statics

Application 3.1

Consider a market where the demand and supply relations are given by

$$p = a - bx \qquad\qquad \text{Demand}$$
$$p = c + dx \qquad\qquad \text{Supply}$$

where p denotes market price and x denotes quantity. Assume also that the parameters a, b, c, and d are all strictly positive. Note that since $b > 0$ and $d > 0$, demand slopes downward and supply slopes upward as we expect. We compute the market equilibrium price $p*$ and quantity $x*$ by setting demand equal to supply, yielding

$$p^* = \frac{ad + bc}{b + d}$$
$$x^* = \frac{a - c}{b + d}$$

Observe that since quantities must be nonnegative, the model is meaningful only if $a \geq c$. Most importantly, note that the *equilibrium* price $p*$ and quantity $x*$ are functions of the parameters a, b, c, and d. In general, the values of a and b are determined by factors such as consumer income and the prices of goods that are complements with and substitutes for x. The values of c and d will be determined by input prices and the state of technology, etc. A change in any one of these things will change one or more of the parameter values and hence induce a change in $p*$ and $x*$. The eight partial derivatives

$$\frac{\partial p^*}{\partial a} = \frac{d}{b + d} > 0 \qquad\qquad \frac{\partial p^*}{\partial b} = \frac{d(c - a)}{(b + d)^2} < 0$$

$$\frac{\partial p^*}{\partial c} = \frac{b}{b + d} > 0 \qquad\qquad \frac{\partial p^*}{\partial d} = \frac{b(a - c)}{(b + d)^2} > 0$$

$$\frac{\partial x^*}{\partial a} = \frac{1}{b + d} > 0 \qquad\qquad \frac{\partial x^*}{\partial b} = \frac{c - a}{(b + d)^2} < 0$$

$$\frac{\partial x^*}{\partial c} = \frac{-1}{b + d} < 0 \qquad\qquad \frac{\partial x^*}{\partial d} = \frac{c - a}{(b + d)^2} < 0$$

are the comparative statics derivatives of the model. They show the *direction* (increase or decrease) and the *rate* of change of the *equilibrium* price and quantity as the parameters of the model vary.

As an example, suppose the parameter c denotes the wage rate that producers of x must pay their employees. We know that in general an increase in any input price will shift firms' supply curves to the left. We observe, then, that an exogenously induced increase in the wage rate will increase the equilibrium price and decrease the corresponding equilibrium quantity as illustrated in Figure 3.1. This reflects the fact that $\partial p^*/\partial c > 0$ and $\partial x^*/\partial c < 0$.

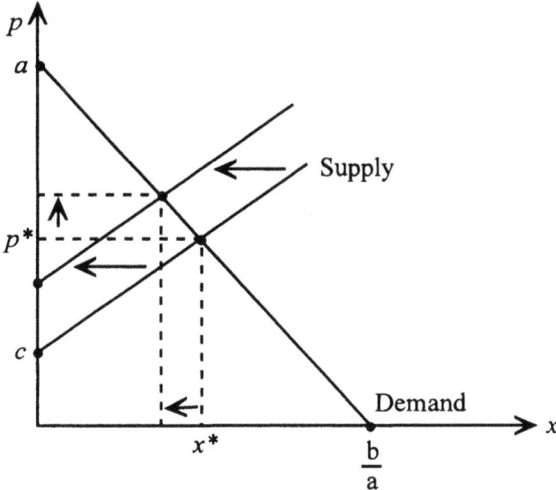

Figure 3.1

Applying this model to a specific market, the testable hypotheses are of two types. First, *assuming* linearity of the demand and supply relationships, what are the values of a, b, c, and d? Second, and more generally, is the assumption of linearity of demand and supply valid? In other words, would quadratic or some other functional forms more accurately represent demand and supply in this market?

3.3 Comparative Statics with Unconstrained Optimization

Application 3.2

Consider a firm producing an output y from input x according to the production function $y = Ax^{\frac{1}{2}}$, where $A > 0$. A represents all the influences, *other than x*, that determine y. Changes in the value of A over time reflect "technical progress." In general, A could be expected to increase over time. Figure 3.2 illustrates the production function when $A = 1$ and $A = 2$.

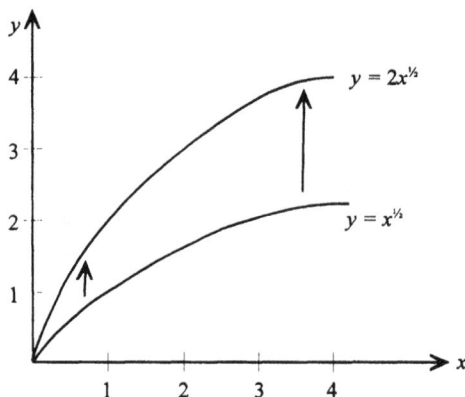

Figure 3.2

As A increases, the output level associated with each value of $x > 0$ increases.

Suppose that the market price of output y is \$2 per unit and that the firm pays \$1 for each unit of input x. Then the firm's profit function is $\pi(x) = 2Ax^{\frac{1}{2}} - x$. We shall assume that the firm selects the input level x^* that maximizes profit. The first-order necessary condition for a profit maximum is

$$\pi'(x) = Ax^{-\frac{1}{2}} - 1 = 0.$$

Solving for x yields $x^* = A^2$. Note that since $\pi''(x) = -\frac{1}{2}Ax^{-3/2} < 0$ at $x = x^*$, $x^* = A^2$ does in fact represent a profit maximum.

Now observe that the profit maximizing input level is a function of the parameter A, i.e., $x^*(A) = A^2$. This function shows how the *optimal* input level varies with the state of technology. Since the comparative statics derivative $dx^*/dA = 2A > 0$, we observe that with input and output prices as stated above, technical progress will induce this firm to employ more of input x. The firm's profit function is shown in Figure 3.3 when $A = 1$ and $A = 2$.

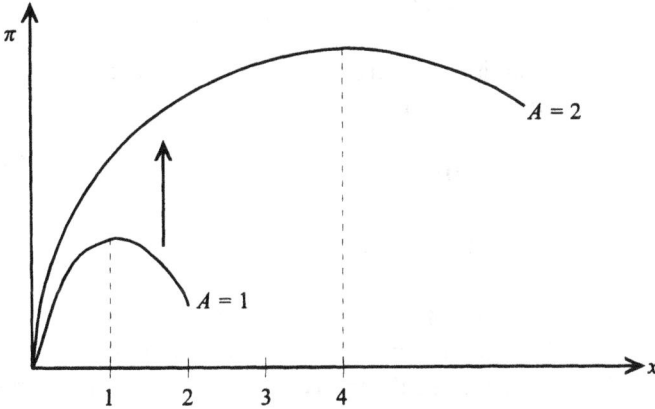

Figure 3.3

The diagram illustrates the fact that as A increases, the profit function is shifted upward for all $x > 0$. Moreover, as A increases, the profit maximizing level of x increases: $x^*(1) = 1$, $x^*(2) = 4$. Thus, the diagram reflects the fact that $dx^*/dA > 0$.

Application 3.3

Consider a monopoly that produces its output y in two separate plants. Let y_i denote the output level of plant i, $i = 1, 2$. The cost functions are $c_1(y_1) = y_1^2$ for plant one and $c_2(y_2) = y_2^2/2$ for plant two. The output $y = y_1 + y_2$ is sold in a market where the demand curve is given by $p = M - y$ where p denotes price and M denotes consumer income. We shall investigate how changes in consumer income affect the profit maximizing production level in each plant.

The firm's total sales revenue $R = yp = yM - y^2$. Since $y = y_1 + y_2$, we obtain

$$R = M(y_1 + y_2) - y_1^2 - 2y_1y_2 - y_2^2.$$

Total production cost is the sum of the costs in each plant: $C = y_1^2 + y_2^2/2$. Profit is therefore

$$\pi = M\left(y_1 + y_2\right) - y_1^2 - 2y_1y_2 - y_2^2 - y_1^2 - \frac{y_2^2}{2}. \tag{1}$$

To find the profit maximizing production level for each plant, set the partial derivatives of (1) equal to zero:

$$\pi_1 = M - 2y_1 - 2y_2 - 2y_1 = 0$$

$$\pi_2 = M - 2y_1 - 2y_2 - y_2 = 0.$$

These equations state that optimality requires that the marginal cost in each plant must equal the marginal revenue for the monopoly as a whole, i.e., $MR = MC_1 = MC_2$. Solving simultaneously yields $y_1^* = M/8$ and $y_2^* = M/4$. Forming the relevant Hessian matrix

$$H = \begin{bmatrix} \pi_{11} & \pi_{12} \\ \pi_{21} & \pi_{22} \end{bmatrix} = \begin{bmatrix} -4 & -2 \\ -2 & -3 \end{bmatrix},$$

observe that since $-4 < 0$ and $|H| = 8 > 0$, the point (y_1^*, y_2^*) does indeed represent a profit maximum. The monopolist's total output is $y^* = y_1^* + y_2^* = 3M/8$, with $M/8$ units produced in plant one and $M/4$ units produced in plant two. Furthermore, since demand is $p = M - y$, when $y^* = 3M/8$, $p^* = 5M/8$.

Consider now the effect of an increase in M. The comparative statics derivatives are

$$\frac{dy_1^*}{dM} = \frac{1}{8} > 0 \qquad\qquad \frac{dy_2^*}{dM} = \frac{1}{4} > 0$$

$$\frac{dy^*}{dM} = \frac{3}{8} > 0 \qquad\qquad \frac{dp^*}{dM} = \frac{5}{8} > 0$$

An increase in consumer income will thus increase the production level in each plant as well as the selling price. Observe also that output increases at a faster rate in plant two than in plant one. This is a consequence of the fact that marginal costs rise slower in plant two than in plant one. Figure 3.4 provides an illustration. To depict the profit maximizing situation graphically, add the two plants' marginal cost curves *horizontally*, obtaining the curve in the diagram denoted by MC. The output level for which $MR = MC$ is the profit maximizing output level for the monopoly as a whole. The MC_1 and MC_2 curves then reveal the output levels that are optimal for each plant. Note that $MC_1 (y_1^*) = MC_2(y_2^*) = MR(y^*)$ as required for profit maximization.

To illustrate the effect of an increase in M, note first that since $R = yM - y^2$, $MR = M - 2y$. Therefore, an increase in M induces a parallel shift in MR to the right, increasing y^*, y_1^*, and y_2^*. As we asserted on the basis of our computations of dy_1^*/dM and dy_2^*/dM, the diagram shows that for a given increase in M, the largest increase in output comes from plant two, where MC rises the slowest. Indeed, if we denote the change in M by $\Delta M > 0$, then using the formulas for y_1^* and y_2^* we obtain $\Delta y_1^* = \Delta M/8$ and $\Delta y_2^* = \Delta M/4$. Since $\Delta M/4 > \Delta M/8$, we have $\Delta y_2^* > \Delta y_1^*$.

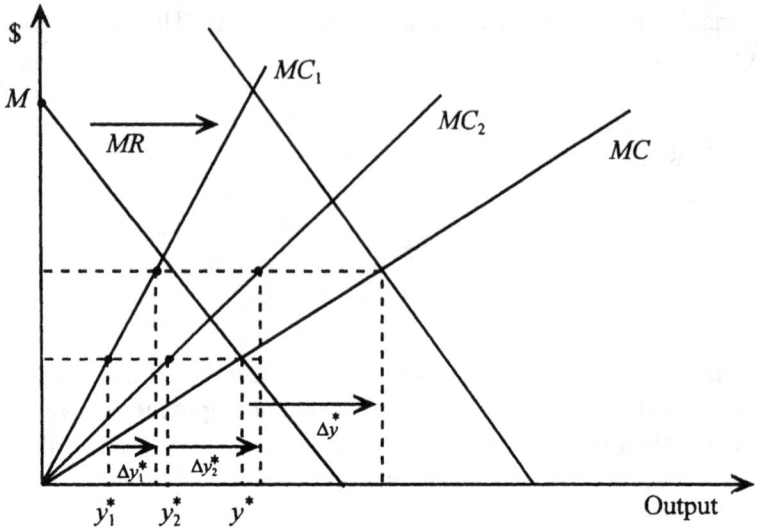

Figure 3.4

3.4. Comparative Statics with Constrained Optimization

Application 3.4

Suppose that an automobile tire manufacturer produces two grades of tires, A and B. This firm can produce x_1 (hundred) grade A tires and x_2 (hundred) grade B tires per day at a cost of

$$C(x_1, x_2) = 3x_1^2 - 2x_1x_2 + x_2^2$$

Suppose further that the tire manufacturer is under contract to produce a total of T tires per day in any combination, i.e., $x_1 + x_2 = T$. We shall determine the optimal number of tires of each grade that should be produced if the firm wishes to fulfill its contract at least cost.

First form the Lagrangian function

$$L(x_1, x_2, \lambda) = 3x_1^2 - 2x_1x_2 + x_2^2 + \lambda[T - x_1 - x_2].$$

The first-order necessary conditions for a constrained minimum of $C(x_1, x_2)$ are

$$L_1 = 6x_1 - 2x_2 - \lambda = 0$$

$$L_2 = -2x_1 + 2x_2 - \lambda = 0 \tag{2}$$

$$L_\lambda = T - x_1 - x_2 = 0.$$

Since $6x_1 - 2x_2 = \partial C/\partial x_1$ and $-2x_1 + 2x_2 = \partial C/\partial x_2$, the first two equations tell us that optimality requires that the marginal cost of each grade of tire be equated. Solving this system of three equations and three unknowns yields:

$$x_1^* = T/3 \qquad x_2^* = 2T/3 \qquad \lambda^* = 2T/3$$

To confirm that we have found a constrained minimum, let $g(x_1. x_2) = T - x_1 - x_2$ and form the bordered Hessian

$$H = \begin{bmatrix} L_{11} & L_{12} & g_1 \\ L_{21} & L_{22} & g_2 \\ g_1 & g_2 & 0 \end{bmatrix} = \begin{bmatrix} 6 & -2 & -1 \\ -2 & 2 & -1 \\ -1 & -1 & 0 \end{bmatrix}.$$

Since $|H| = -12 < 0$, the second-order sufficient condition for a constrained minimum is satisfied at $(x_1^*, x_2^*, \lambda^*)$.

The firm's cost minimization problem is illustrated in Figure 3.5.

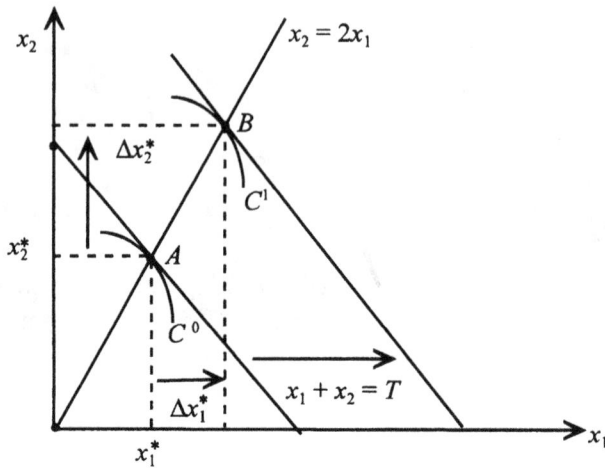

Figure 3.5

The contract requires the firm to satisfy $x_1 + x_2 = T$. The firm's *isocost* curves are all curves of the form

$$3x_1^2 - 2x_1x_2 + x_2^2 = \text{constant}.$$

Cost increases as we move upward and to the right in the diagram. The firm wants to be on the lowest isocost curve that has a point in common with the line $x_1 + x_2 = T$. This is a tangency point, occurring at (x_1^*, x_2^*) in Figure 3.5. The curve labeled C^0 is the isocost curve passing through the cost minimizing point.

Now, since $x_1^* = T/3$ and $x_2^* = 2T/3$, we observe that for any value of T, $x_2^* = 2x_1^*$. This implies that the solution to the firm's cost minimization problem *always* lies along the line $x_2 = 2x_1$. Therefore, any variation in the number of tires contracted for induces the firm to expand or contract its production along this line. Suppose, for example, that T increases, shifting the constraint to the right as indicated in the diagram. The cost minimizing point moves from point A to B. The curve labeled C^1 is the isocost curve passing through the new optimum. Since $x_1^* = T/3$ and $x_2^* = 2T/3$, the comparative statics derivatives are

$$\frac{dx_1^*}{dT} = 1/3 \qquad\qquad \frac{dx_2^*}{dT} = 2/3.$$

This implies that if T increases by $\Delta T > 0$, $\Delta x_1^* = \Delta T/3$ and $\Delta x_2^* = 2\Delta T/3$. Hence, two-thirds of the additional tires produced are grade B and one-third are grade A.

Application 3.5

Consider a consumer who consumes two commodities, x and y and has preferences represented by the utility function $u(x, y) = ln(x) + y$, where $ln(\cdot)$ denotes the natural log function. This utility function belongs to a class of functions known as *quasilinear functions* since they are linear functions of one commodity. Assume that the price of x is p, the price of y is one, and income is M. The consumer chooses consumption levels of each commodity to maximize utility subject to the budget constraint, i.e.,

Maximize $ln(x) + y$
$\quad x, y$
subject to $px + y = M$.

We shall investigate how these optimal consumption levels are affected by changes in the parameter M.

We begin by forming the Lagrangian function

$$L(x, y, \lambda) = ln(x) + y + \lambda\left[M - px - y\right].$$

The first-order necessary conditions for a constrained maximum of $u(x, y)$ are

$$L_1 = \frac{1}{x} - \lambda p = 0$$

$$L_2 = 1 - \lambda = 0$$

$$L_\lambda = M - px - y = 0$$

where we use the fact that when $f(x) = ln(x)$, $f'(x) = 1/x$. Solving this system of three equations and three unknowns yields

$$x^* = 1/p \quad y^* = M - 1, \quad \lambda^* = 1.$$

To establish this point as a maximum subject to the constraint $g(x, y) = M - px - y = 0,$, form the *bordered Hessian*

$$H = \begin{bmatrix} L_{11} & L_{12} & g_1 \\ L_{21} & L_{22} & g_2 \\ g_1 & g_2 & 0 \end{bmatrix} = \begin{bmatrix} -1/x^2 & 0 & -p \\ 0 & 0 & -1 \\ -p & -1 & 0 \end{bmatrix}.$$

Now, $|H| = 1/x^2$. Evaluating at the point x^* yields $|H| = p^2 > 0$. Hence, the second-order sufficient condition for a constrained maximum is satisfied at (x^*, y^*, λ^*).

The functions x^* and y^* are this consumer's *Marshallian Demand Functions*, which, in general, express the utility maximizing consumption choices in terms of prices and income. In this particular case, we observe that the consumer's demand for x is independent of M and the demand for y is independent of the price of x. (The significance of the Lagrange multiplier will be discussed in Chapter 5).

The consumer's utility maximization problem is illustrated in Figure 3.6.

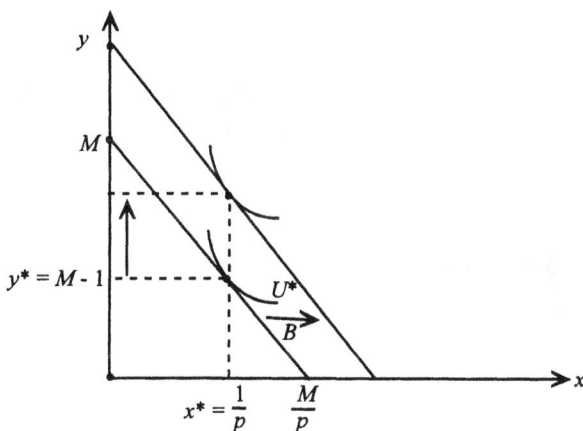

Figure 3.6

For any budget line B, the consumer desires to be on the highest indifference curve that has a point in common with B. As was the case in Application 3.4, the solution is a tangency point. The indifference curve labeled U^* passes through the utility maximizing point.

Now an increase in the parameter M shifts the budget line to the right in a parallel fashion, giving a new utility maximization point. Since x^* does not depend on M, x^* is unchanged. Since $y^* = M - 1$, we have $\Delta y^* = \Delta M$, implying that all additional income is spent on y.

This model is particularly useful when modeling a situation where one commodity, x, involves a very small fraction of a person's total budget. The other commodity, y, may then be thought of as money spent on all commodities *other than x*. For example, suppose x = toothpaste. If a consumer experiences an increase in income, it is likely that his consumption of toothpaste would remain the same and that the additional income would be spent on other commodities. Conversely, the quasilinear model would probably not accurately represent the behavior of a consumer if x represented an item that was a more significant share of the total budget, such as entertainment, food, or clothing. Many people could be expected to increase their consumption of these items if they were to experience an income increase.

Problems

1. Consider a market where demand and supply are

   $p = M - x$ Demand

   $p = \dfrac{x}{2}$ Supply

   where M denotes consumer income.

   a. Graph the demand and supply curves, assuming that $M \geq p$.
   b. Compute the equlibrium price p^* and quantity x^*. How are they affected by a change in M?
   c. Illustrate graphically the effect of an increase in M.

2. A ship is to make a trip between two ports, A and B. The cost per hour of operating the ship is $C = w + v^n$, where $w > 0$ denotes the wages of the ship's employees, v denotes the ship's velocity through the water, and $n > 1$. The trip is to be made at minimum cost.

   a. Use the fact that (velocity) × (time) = distance to show that the cost minimizing velocity is

   $$v^* = \left(\frac{w}{n - 1} \right)^{1/n}$$

   b. How is v^* affected by an exogenous change in w?

3. Consider a monopolist with the demand curve $p = a - by$ where y denotes quantity and a and b are positive constants. The monopolist's average variable cost is $AVC = c$ and fixed cost is $F \geq 0$.

   a. What is the monopolist's profit function?
   b. Determine the profit maximizing quantity y^* and corresponding price p^*.
   c. How are p^* and y^* affected if c increases?
   d. Illustrate graphically.

4. Consider a monopolist with demand and cost functions given by

$$p = a - by \qquad\qquad C = cy + F$$

where a, b, c, $F > 0$ and y denotes output. Suppose that the government imposes a tax of $\$t$ per unit of output produced and sold.

a. Determine the firm's (after-tax) profit function.
b. Determine the profit maximizing output level y^* and corresponding price p^*.
c. How are they affected by an increase in the tax parameter?
d. Illustrate in a diagram showing MR, MC, and demand.

5. A farmer has F feet of fence with which to enclose a (rectangular) garden. He wants the area of the garden to be as large as possible.

a. Compute the optimal dimensions of the garden.
b. How much longer should each side be made if the farmer obtains four additional feet of fence?

6. Suppose that a firm produces two *outputs*, y_1 and y_2 from a single input x according to the production function $x = y_1^2 + y_2^2$. The (competitive) output prices are p_1 and p_2. The price of input x is w, implying that the firm's total cost is wx.

a. Determine the firm's profit function $\pi(y_1, y_2)$.
b. Compute the profit maximizing input and output levels x^*, y_1^*, and y_2^*.
c. How are each of these optimal values affected by changes in p_1, p_2, and w?
d. Is the firm's input demand reduced when w increases?

7. Consider a firm that produces output y from inputs x_1 and x_2 according to the production function

$$y = \sqrt{x_1 x_2}.$$

The input prices are w_1 and w_2, and the firm has a fixed budget of C dollars. The firm desires to maximize *output* subject to the budget constraint $w_1 x_1 + w_2 x_2 = C$.

   a. Compute the firm's input demand functions $x_1^*(w_1, w_2, C)$ and $x_2^*(w_1, w_2, C)$. How are they affected by changes in w_1, w_2, and C?

   b. Let y^* denote the corresponding output level. How is y^* affected by changes in w_1, w_2, and C?

8. A firm produces output y from input x in two different plants with production functions $y_1 = x_1/2$ and $y_2 = \sqrt{x_2}$ where x_i denotes the amount of the input used in plant i and y_i denotes the amount of output produced in plant i, $i = 1, 2$. The firm has $\bar{x}$ units of the input that may be allocated to either plant: $x_1 + x_2 = \bar{x}$. The firm seeks to maximize total output $y_1 + y_2$.

   a. Determine the optimal input allocation between plants, assuming $\bar{x} > 1$.

   b. How does the allocation change as more x becomes available (i.e., as $\bar{x}$ increases)? Explain intuitively why this must be the case.

4. Comparative Statics in General Function Models

4.1. Introduction to General Function Models

In Chapter 3, we dealt with a series of applications in which the equilibrium or optimal values of the variables were expressible explicitly in terms of the parameters. In these models, ordinary (partial) differentiation was sufficient for obtaining the comparative statics properties of the model. While these explicit solution models do convey the essence of comparative statics analysis, they are of limited value since their comparative statics properties are relevant only for a specific set of functional forms.

In this chapter, we begin our study of general function models. Here the comparative statics derivatives are not available via differentiation of explicit solutions so the implicit methods of Chapter 2 must be employed. In the models based upon an explicit maximization or minimization hypothesis, all comparative statics results are obtained by examining the set of implications of the optimization hypothesis. These implications are the testable hypotheses generated by the models since they generally imply restrictions on *observable* data.

4.2. Equilibrium Comparative Statics

Application 4.1

Consider the market for a commodity x where the demand and supply functions are

$$x^D = D(p, M) \qquad \text{Demand}$$
$$x^S = S(p) \qquad \text{Supply}$$

43

where p denotes market price and M denotes consumer income. The demand and supply functions, which are assumed C^1, satisfy $D_p(p, M) < 0$ and $S'(p) > 0$, reflecting the fact that in general, demand slopes downward and supply slopes upward. For economy of notation, we will denote $D_p(p, M)$ by D_p and $S'(p)$ by S', etc. We assume that for any value of M, an equilibrium exists in this market. We shall examine how the equilibrium price and quantity are affected by exogenously given changes in the parameter M.

Let $F^1(x, p, M) = x - D(p, M)$ and $F^2(x, p, M) = x - S(p)$. The equilibrium conditions in this market are satisfied precisely when

$$F^1(x, p, M) = x - D(p, M) = 0$$
(1)
$$F^2(x, p, M) = x - S(p) = 0$$

since, in this case, $D(p, M) = x = S(p)$. We are interested in solving this system for the equilibrium price and quantity in terms of the parameter M:

$$x = x^*(M)$$

$$p = p^*(M)$$

The Implicit Function Theorem tells us that (1) will define the equilibrium price and quantity as differentiable functions of M provided that

$$|J| = \; = \begin{vmatrix} F_x^1 & F_p^1 \\ F_x^2 & F_p^2 \end{vmatrix} \neq 0 \; .$$

Now, using (1), we obtain $F_x^1 = 1$, $F_p^1 = -D_p$, $F_x^2 = 1$, and $F_p^2 = -S'$. Hence

$$|J| = \begin{vmatrix} 1 & -D_p \\ 1 & -S' \end{vmatrix} = D_p - S' < 0$$

since $S' > 0$ and $D_p < 0$. Therefore, by the Implicit Function Theorem, the functions $x = x^*(M)$ and $p = p^*(M)$ exist, are differentiable, and satisfy the identities

$$F^1\left(x^*(M), p^*(M), M\right) = x^*(M) - D\left(p^*(M), M\right) \equiv 0$$

$$F^2\left(x^*(M), p^*(M), M\right) = x^*(M) - S\left(p^*(M)\right) \equiv 0.$$

The comparative statics derivatives are obtained by differentiating these identities with respect to M:

$$\left(\frac{dx^*}{dM}\right) - D_p\left(\frac{dp^*}{dM}\right) - D_M = 0$$

$$\left(\frac{dx^*}{dM}\right) - S'\left(\frac{dp^*}{dM}\right) = 0.$$

Applying Cramer's Rule to the system

$$\left(\frac{dx^*}{dM}\right) - D_p\left(\frac{dp^*}{dM}\right) = D_M$$

$$\left(\frac{dx^*}{dM}\right) - S'\left(\frac{dp^*}{dM}\right) = 0.$$

yields

$$\frac{dx^*}{dM} = \frac{\begin{vmatrix} D_M & -D_p \\ 0 & -S' \end{vmatrix}}{\begin{vmatrix} 1 & -D_p \\ 1 & -S' \end{vmatrix}} = \frac{-S' \cdot D_M}{D_p - S'} \tag{2}$$

$$\frac{dp^*}{dM} = \frac{\begin{vmatrix} 1 & D_M \\ 1 & 0 \end{vmatrix}}{\begin{vmatrix} 1 & -D_p \\ 1 & -S' \end{vmatrix}} = \frac{-D_M}{D_p - S'}$$ (3)

which are the comparative statics derivatives of the model. Note that these derivatives are well defined precisely because $|J| = D_p - S' \neq 0$. Hence the economic structure of the model (i.e., the laws of supply and demand) insure that the comparative statics derivatives are well defined.

Thus far, we have made no assumption about the nature of the response of demand to income changes, i.e., the sign of D_M. When $D_M > 0$, the good is said to be a *normal good*. In this case, an income increase shifts the demand curve to the right. If $D_M < 0$, the good is an *inferior good*. Observe that if the good is a normal good, using (2) and (3) we have

$$\frac{dp^*}{dM} > 0 \qquad \text{and} \qquad \frac{dx^*}{dM} > 0$$

since, in this case, $D_M > 0$. The comparative statics derivatives therefore tell us that if the good in question is a normal good, an increase in consumer income will cause the equilibrium price and quantity to rise, as illustrated in Figure 4.1.

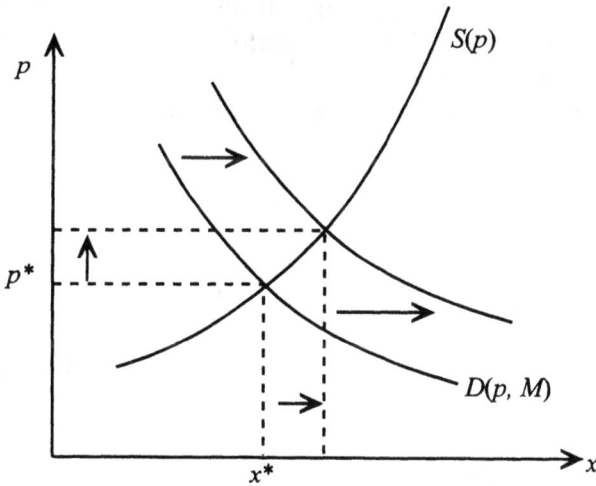

Figure 4.1

(If the good was inferior (i.e., $D_M < 0$), an income increase would shift the demand curve to the left, decreasing the equilibrium price and quantity.) It is important to note that the basic properties of the model – downward sloping demand ($D_p < 0$), upward sloping supply ($S' > 0$), and normality ($D_M > 0$) have allowed us to assert that an income increase must of necessity increase the equilibrium price. No assumptions regarding the functional forms of demand and supply have been made. This model is therefore far more general than the linear model discussed in Chapter 3.

4.3. Comparative Statics with Unconstrained Optimization

Application 4.2

Consider a firm that produces an output y from labor input x. The price of a unit of labor is the (exogenously determined) wage rate denoted by w. The firm's cost function $C(w, y)$ gives the *minimum* cost of producing output level y when the wage rate is w. The firm's marginal cost is $C_y(w, y)$, which we denote by

$MC(w, y)$ and average cost is $C(w, y)/y$, denoted by $AC(w, y)$. We assume that $MC(w, y)$ and $AC(w, y)$ are C^1. It is straightforward to show that when $MC < AC$, AC is a decreasing function of y and that when $MC > AC$, AC is an increasing function of y. It is often the case that a firm's average cost curve is U-shaped, as depicted in Figure 4.2.

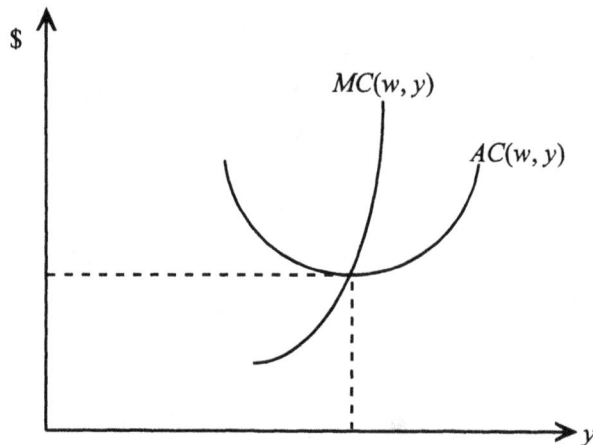

Figure 4.2

Consistent with Figure 4.2, we shall assume that $MC_y > 0$, i.e., marginal cost is an increasing function of output. The above mentioned relationship between the marginal and the average implies that $MC = AC$ at the output level for which AC is minimum.

The output level where AC is minimum is often quite important. Indeed, in microeconomic theory, one learns that the long-run equilibrium position of a perfectly competitive market involves each firm producing the output level for which AC is minimum. In this application, we will examine how this output level is affected by changes in w.

In general, an increase in w will shift the average and marginal cost curves upward. We shall therefore assume $AC_w > 0$ and $MC_w > 0$. Now the output level at which average cost is minimum is the output level that satisfies

$$MC(w, y) = AC(w, y). \tag{4}$$

Define $F(w, y) = MC(w, y) - AC(w, y)$. For any value of w, the output level that satisfies $F(w, y) = 0$ is the output level at which AC is minimum. We are interested in solving this equation for the output level in terms of parameter w: $y = y^*(w)$.

The Implicit Function Theorem tells us that as long as $F_y \neq 0$, the output level at which average cost is minimum is a differentiable function of w. Now $F_y = MC_y - AC_y$. Since $AC_y = 0$ when average cost is minimized, we have $F_y = MC_y > 0$ and hence the hypothesis of the Implicit Function Theorem is satisfied. Therefore, the output level that solves (4) may be expressed as a differentiable function of w, $y = y^*(w)$. Moreover, this function satisfies the identity $F\big(w, y^*(w)\big) \equiv 0$ or, equivalently

$$MC\big(w, y^*(w)\big) \equiv AC\big(w, y^*(w)\big).$$

Differentiating with respect to w we obtain

$$MC_w + MC_y \cdot \frac{dy^*}{dw} = AC_w + AC_y \cdot \frac{dy^*}{dw}.$$

Using the fact that $AC_y = 0$ when average cost is minimum, the comparative statics derivative is

$$\frac{dy^*}{dw} = \frac{AC_w - MC_w}{MC_y}.$$

Since $MC_y > 0$ by assumption, $dy^*/dw > 0$ when $AC_w > MC_w$ and $dy^*/dw < 0$ when $AC_w < MC_w$. AC_w and MC_w measure the (marginal) increase in AC and MC when w increases. If $AC_w > MC_w$, the AC curve is shifting upward by more than the MC curve and so y^* increases, as depicted in Figure 4.3.

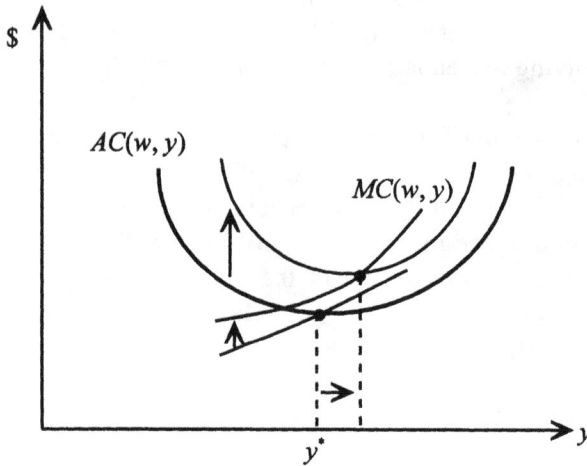

Figure 4.3

Note that if $AC_w = MC_w$, AC and MC shift vertically by the same amount. In this case, the output level at which $MC = AC$ remains fixed, as can be confirmed by a careful geometric argument.

Application 4.3

Consider a monopoly that produces its output y in two separate plants. The cost functions for each plant are $c_1(y_1)$ and $c_2(y_2)$ where y_i denotes the output level in plant i, $i = 1, 2$. It is assumed that these cost functions are C^2 and satisfy $c_i' > 0$ and $c_i'' > 0$ for all $y_i \geq 0$, $i = 1, 2$. The output $y = y_1 + y_2$ is sold in a market where the demand function is $p(y)$, where p denotes price. The firm's total revenue is $R(y) = p(y) \cdot y$. We also assume R is C^2 and satisfies $R' > 0$ and $R'' < 0$ for all $y \geq 0$.

Suppose that the government imposes a sales tax of t dollars per unit of output. Then

$$\pi = R\left(y_1 + y_2\right) - c_1\left(y_1\right) - c_2\left(y_2\right) - t \cdot \left(y_1 + y_2\right). \tag{5}$$

In this exercise, we examine how the profit maximizing output levels in each plant are affected by changes in the tax rate t.

Setting the partial derivatives of (5) equal to zero, we obtain

$$R'(y) - c_1'(y_1) - t = 0$$
$$R'(y) - c_2'(y_2) - t = 0. \tag{6}$$

Thus, profit maximization requires that the after-tax marginal revenue for the monopoly as a whole must equal the marginal cost in each plant. Now form the Hessian matrix

$$H = \begin{bmatrix} R'' - c_1'' & R'' \\ R'' & R'' - c_2'' \end{bmatrix}.$$

The second-order sufficient conditions, which are assumed to hold, require that $R'' - c_1'' < 0$ and $|H| > 0$ at the point where (6) holds.

Now define

$$F^1(y_1, y_2, t) = R'(y_1 + y_2) - c'_1(y_1) - t$$
and
$$F^2(y_1, y_2, t) = R'(y_1 + y_2) - c'_2(y_2) - t.$$

Profit is maximized precisely when

$$F^1(y_1, y_2, t) = 0$$
$$F^2(y_1, y_2, t) = 0, \tag{7}$$

assuming the second-order conditions hold. We desire to solve this system of equations for the profit maximizing output levels in terms of the tax parameter:

$y_1 = y_1^*(t)$

$y_2 = y_2^*(t).$

By the Implicit Function Theorem, (7) will define the profit maximizing output levels as differentiable functions of t provided that

$$|J| = \begin{vmatrix} F_1^1 & F_2^1 \\ F_1^2 & F_2^2 \end{vmatrix} \neq 0 \ .$$

Now, using the definitions of F and G, we have

$$F_1^1 = R'' - c_1'' \qquad F_2^1 = R''$$

$$F_1^2 = R'' \qquad F_2^2 = R'' - c_2''$$

Thus

$$|J| = \begin{vmatrix} R'' - c_1'' & R'' \\ R'' & R'' - c_2'' \end{vmatrix} > 0$$

as a consequence of the second-order conditions. This conclusion reflects a general truth whose importance cannot be overstated: In an optimization-based model, if the first-order necessary and second-order sufficient conditions are satisfied at a particular point, then the first-order necessary conditions can be solved (in principle) for the optimal values of the variables as differentiable functions of the parameters.

Since $|J| \neq 0$, the Implicit Function Theorem insures that the functions $y_1 = y_1^*(t)$ and $y_2 = y_2^*(t)$ exist, are differentiable, and satisfy the identities

$$F^1\left(y_1^*(t), y_2^*(t), t\right) = R'\left(y_1^*(t) + y_2^*(t)\right) - c_1'\left(y_1^*(t)\right) - t \equiv 0$$

$$F^2\left(y_1^*(t),y_2^*(t),t\right) = R'\left(y_1^*(t)+y_2^*(t)\right) - c_2'\left(y_2^*(t)\right) - t \equiv 0.$$

To obtain the comparative statics derivatives $\dfrac{dy_1^*}{dt}$ and $\dfrac{dy_2^*}{dt}$, differentiate these identities with respect to t:

$$R'' \cdot \left(\frac{dy_1^*}{dt} + \frac{dy_2^*}{dt}\right) - c_1'' \cdot \frac{dy_1^*}{dt} - 1 = 0$$

$$R'' \cdot \left(\frac{dy_1^*}{dt} + \frac{dy_2^*}{dt}\right) - c_2'' \cdot \frac{dy_2^*}{dt} - 1 = 0.$$

Rearranging terms, we have

$$\frac{dy_1^*}{dt} \cdot \left(R'' - c_1''\right) + \frac{dy_2^*}{dt} \cdot \left(R''\right) = 1$$

$$\frac{dy_1^*}{dt} \cdot \left(R''\right) + \frac{dy_2^*}{dt} \cdot \left(R'' - c_2''\right) = 1.$$

Applying Cramer's Rule, we obtain

$$\frac{dy_1^*}{dt} = \frac{\begin{vmatrix} 1 & R'' \\ 1 & R'' - c_2'' \end{vmatrix}}{\begin{vmatrix} R'' - c_1'' & R'' \\ R'' & R'' - c_2'' \end{vmatrix}} = \frac{-c_2''}{|J|} < 0$$

and

$$\frac{dy_2^*}{dt} = \frac{\begin{vmatrix} R'' - c_1'' & 1 \\ R'' & 1 \end{vmatrix}}{\begin{vmatrix} R'' - c_1'' & R'' \\ R'' & R'' - c_2'' \end{vmatrix}} = \frac{-c_1''}{|J|} < 0$$

since $|J| > 0$. Therefore, we observe that an increase in the tax rate will decrease the output level in each plant. Note also that $dy_1^*/dt < dy_2^*/dt$ if and only if $c_2'' > c_1''$. This implies that when the tax rate increases, the largest reduction in output occurs in the plant where marginal cost rises most slowly.

4.4. Comparative Statics with Constrained Optimization

Application 4.4

In models of consumer behavior such as the one discussed in Application 3.5, the consumer's income was assumed to be exogenously determined, i.e., it enters the utility maximization problem as a parameter, which we denoted by M. In general equilibrium analysis however, the consumer is often assumed to possess *initial endowments* of the goods. These are simply the quantities of the goods that the consumer "brings to the market," where he/she is free to buy or sell at market prices. His/her "income" is the market value of his/her endowment and therefore depends on the values of the prices. The budget constraint requires that the market value of his/her purchases equals the market value of his/her endowment.

In this application, we study utility maximization when income is determined by endowments. We assume there are two commodities x and y, and the consumer has the *additively separable* utility function

$$U(x, y) = u_1(x) + u_2(y)$$

where $u'_i > 0$, $u''_i < 0$, $i = 1, 2$. Marginal utilities are thus assumed positive but diminishing. Additively separable utility functions are frequently used in empirical work.

The consumer has an endowment vector $(\bar{x}, \bar{y})$ with $\bar{x} > 0$ and $\bar{y} > 0$. The market prices of x and y are p and q, respectively. The consumer solves

Maximize $\quad u_1(x) + u_2(y)$
x, y

subject to $px + qy = p\bar{x} + q\bar{y}$.

We shall examine how the utility maximizing consumption choices are affected by changes in the value of the endowment parameter $\bar{x}$.

Form the Lagrangian Function

$$L(x, y, \lambda) = u_1(x) + u_2(y) + \lambda \left[p\bar{x} + q\bar{y} - px - qy \right].$$

The first-order necessary conditions for a constrained utility maximum are

$$L_x = u'_1(x) - \lambda p = 0$$
$$L_y = u'_2(y) - \lambda q = 0$$
$$L_\lambda = p\bar{x} + q\bar{y} - px - qy = 0.$$

Now, let $g(x, y) = p\bar{x} + q\bar{y} - px - qy$ and form the bordered Hessian

$$H = \begin{bmatrix} L_{11} & L_{12} & g_1 \\ L_{21} & L_{22} & g_2 \\ g_1 & g_2 & 0 \end{bmatrix} = \begin{bmatrix} u''_1 & 0 & -p \\ 0 & u''_2 & -q \\ -p & -q & 0 \end{bmatrix}.$$

Since $|H| = -q^2 u_1'' - p^2 u_2'' > 0$, the second-order sufficient condition for a constrained maximum holds at any point where (8) holds.

Now define

$$F^1(x, y, \lambda, \bar{x}) = u_1'(x) - \lambda p$$

$$F^2(x, y, \lambda, \bar{x}) = u_2'(y) - \lambda q$$

and

$$F^3(x, y, \lambda, \bar{x}) = p\bar{x} + q\bar{y} - px - qy.$$

Utility is maximized subject to the budget constraint precisely when

$$F^1(x, y, \lambda, \bar{x}) = 0$$

$$F^2(x, y, \lambda, \bar{x}) = 0$$

and   (9)

$$F^3(x, y, \lambda, \bar{x}) = 0.$$

We want to solve this system of equations for the utility maximizing consumption levels and the Lagrange multiplier in terms of the endowment parameter $\bar{x}$:

$$x = x^*(\bar{x})$$

$$y = y^*(\bar{x})$$

$$\lambda = \lambda^*(\bar{x}).$$

By the Implicit Function Theorem (9) will define these functions provided that

$$|J| = \begin{vmatrix} F_x^1 & F_y^1 & F_\lambda^1 \\ F_x^2 & F_y^2 & F_\lambda^2 \\ F_x^3 & F_y^3 & F_\lambda^3 \end{vmatrix} \neq 0 \quad .$$

Now, using the definitions of F^1, F^2, and F^3, we have

$$F^1_x = u''_1 \quad F^1_y = 0 \quad F^1_\lambda = -p$$

$$F^2_x = 0 \quad F^2_y = u''_2 \quad F^2_\lambda = -q$$

$$F^3_x = -p \quad F^3_y = -q \quad F^3_\lambda = 0$$

Hence

$$|J| = \begin{vmatrix} u''_1 & 0 & -p \\ 0 & u''_2 & -q \\ -p & -q & 0 \end{vmatrix} > 0$$

as a consequence of the second-order condition. The statement made in Application 4.3 applies in the case of constrained optimization as well: If the first-order necessary and second-order sufficient conditions are satisfied at a particular point, then the first-order conditions can be solved for the optimal values of the variables as differentiable functions of the parameters.

Since $|J| \neq 0$, the Implicit Function Theorem insures that the functions $x = x^*(\bar{x})$, $y = y^*(\bar{x})$, and $\lambda = \lambda^*(\bar{x})$ exist, are differentiable, and satisfy the identities

$$F^1\left(x^*(\bar{x}), y^*(\bar{x}), \lambda^*(\bar{x}), \bar{x}\right) = u'_1\left(x^*(\bar{x})\right) - \lambda^*(\bar{x})p \equiv 0$$

$$F^2\left(x^*(\bar{x}), y^*(\bar{x}), \lambda^*(\bar{x}), \bar{x}\right) = u'_2\left(y^*(\bar{x})\right) - \lambda^*(\bar{x})q \equiv 0$$

$$F^3\left(x^*(\bar{x}), y^*(\bar{x}), \lambda^*(\bar{x}), \bar{x}\right) = p\bar{x} + q\bar{y} - px^*(\bar{x}) - qy^*(\bar{x}) \equiv 0.$$

To obtain the comparative statics derivatives $dx^*/d\bar{x}$, $dy^*/d\bar{x}$, and $d\lambda^*/d\bar{x}$, differentiate these identities with respect to $\bar{x}$:

$$u_1'' \cdot \frac{dx^*}{dx} - p \cdot \frac{d\lambda^*}{dx} = 0$$

$$u_2'' \cdot \frac{dy^*}{dx} - q \cdot \frac{d\lambda^*}{dx} = 0$$

$$p - p \cdot \frac{dx^*}{dx} - q \cdot \frac{dy^*}{dx} = 0 \ .$$

Rearranging terms and emphasizing the structure of the system, we have

$$u_1'' \cdot \left(\frac{dx^*}{dx} \right) + 0 \cdot \left(\frac{dy^*}{dx} \right) - p \cdot \left(\frac{d\lambda^*}{dx} \right) = 0$$

$$0 \cdot \left(\frac{dx^*}{dx} \right) + u_2'' \cdot \left(\frac{dy^*}{dx} \right) - q \cdot \left(\frac{d\lambda^*}{dx} \right) = 0$$

$$- p \cdot \left(\frac{dx^*}{dx} \right) - q \cdot \left(\frac{dy^*}{dx} \right) + 0 \cdot \left(\frac{d\lambda^*}{dx} \right) = - p \ .$$

Applying Cramer's Rule, we obtain the comparative statics derivatives:

$$\frac{dx^*}{dx} = \frac{\begin{vmatrix} 0 & 0 & -p \\ 0 & u_2'' & -q \\ -p & -q & 0 \end{vmatrix}}{\begin{vmatrix} u_1'' & 0 & -p \\ 0 & u_2'' & -q \\ -p & -q & 0 \end{vmatrix}} = \frac{-p^2 \cdot u_2''}{|J|} > 0$$

$$\frac{dy^*}{dx} = \frac{\begin{vmatrix} u_1'' & 0 & -p \\ 0 & 0 & -q \\ -p & -p & 0 \end{vmatrix}}{\begin{vmatrix} u_1'' & 0 & -p \\ 0 & u_2'' & -q \\ -p & -q & 0 \end{vmatrix}} = \frac{-p \cdot q \cdot u_1''}{|J|} > 0$$

and

$$\frac{d\lambda^*}{dx} = \frac{\begin{vmatrix} u_1'' & 0 & 0 \\ 0 & u_2'' & 0 \\ -p & -q & -p \end{vmatrix}}{\begin{vmatrix} u_1'' & 0 & -p \\ 0 & u_2'' & -q \\ -p & -q & 0 \end{vmatrix}} = \frac{-p \cdot u_1'' \cdot u_2''}{|J|} < 0$$

since $|J| > 0$. Therefore, an increase in $\bar{x}$ will increase consumption of x *and* y. (Again, the significance of the comparative statics derivative $d\lambda^*/d\bar{x}$ will be discussed in Chapter 5.)

The model is illustrated in Figure 4.4.

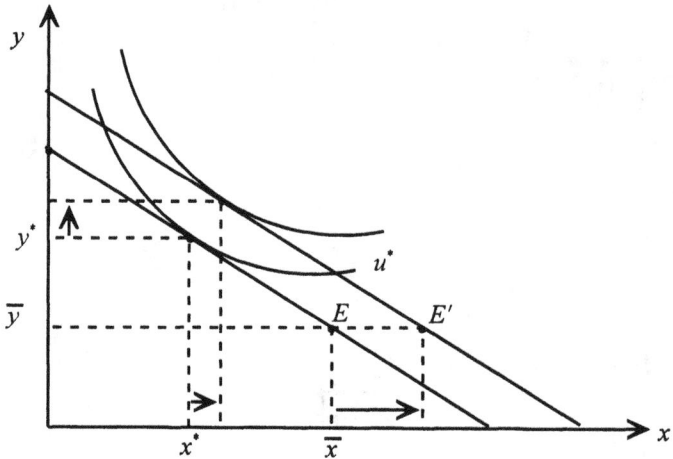

Figure 4.4

The endowment is denoted by point E. The diagram depicts a situation where the consumer sells $\bar{x}$ - x^* units of x and purchases y^* - $\bar{y}$ additional units of y. The indifference curve passing through the utility maximizing point is labeled u^*. If the endowment of good x increases, the new endowment point is E'. The budget line therefore shifts in a parallel fashion to the right. The utility maximizing consumption levels of x and y both increase since $dx^*/d\bar{x} > 0$ and $dy^*/d\bar{x} > 0$. (Note: The point (x^*, y^*) *could* be below and to the right of E along the original budget line. If this were the case, the consumer would be selling y and purchasing x. Nevertheless, an increase in $\bar{x}$ would still increase x^* and y^*.)

Application 4.5

Consider a firm that produces output y from inputs x_1 and x_2 according to the C^2 production function $y = f(x_1, x_2)$, where $f_1, f_2 > 0$. The price of input one is w_1, but the price of input two is subject to uncertainty. Specifically, assume that the price of a unit of input two can realize one of two distinct values $\left(w_2^L, w_2^H \right)$ with the respective probabilities $(\pi, 1 - \pi)$, where $0 \le \pi \le 1$. Here, w_2^L denotes the "low" price and w_2^H denotes the "high" price, with $w_2^L < w_2^H$. Characterizing the price of input two in this manner makes it a *random variable*.

Now, if $w_2 = w_2^L$, the firm's total production cost is

$$C = w_1 x_1 + w_2^L \cdot x_2$$

and if $w_2 = w_2^H$, total cost is

$$C = w_1 x_1 + w_2^H \cdot x_2.$$

Since the probability that $w_2 = w_2^L$ is π and the probability that $w_2 = w_2^H$ is $1 - \pi$, the firm's *expected cost* is

$$E[C] = \pi \left(w_1 x_1 + w_2^L \cdot x_2 \right) + (1 - \pi) \left(w_1 x_1 + w_2^H \cdot x_2 \right)$$

$$= w_1 x_1 + \left(\pi w_2^L + (1 - \pi) w_2^H \right) x_2.$$

Suppose that this firm attempts to produce any output level y at *minimum expected cost*. In this application, we study how the expected cost minimizing input levels are affected by exogenously given changes in the probability parameter π.

The firm solves:

Minimize $E[C]$ subject to $y = f(x_1, x_2)$
x_1, x_2

From the Lagrangian function

$$L(x_1, x_2, \lambda) = w_1 x_1 + \left(\pi w_2^L + (1 - \pi) w_2^H \right) x_2 + \lambda \left[y - f(x_1, x_2) \right].$$

The first-order necessary conditions for a constrained expected cost minimum are

$$L_1 = w_1 - \lambda f_1(x_1, x_2) = 0$$
$$L_2 = \left(\pi w_2^L + (1 - \pi)w_2^H\right) - \lambda f_2(x_1, x_2) = 0 \tag{10}$$
$$L_\lambda = y - f(x_1, x_2) = 0.$$

Now, let $g(x_1, x_2) = y - f(x_1, x_2)$ and form the bordered Hessian

$$H = \begin{bmatrix} L_{11} & L_{12} & g_1 \\ L_{21} & L_{22} & g_2 \\ g_1 & g_2 & 0 \end{bmatrix} = \begin{bmatrix} -\lambda f_{11} & -\lambda f_{12} & -f_1 \\ -\lambda f_{21} & -\lambda f_{22} & -f_2 \\ -f_1 & -f_2 & 0 \end{bmatrix}.$$

The second-order sufficient condition for a constrained minimum requires

$$|H| = \lambda\left(f_1^2 f_{22} - f_1 f_2 f_{12} - f_1 f_2 f_{21} + f_2^2 f_{11}\right) < 0, \tag{11}$$

which we assume is satisfied. (If the production function generates isoquants with the "convex" shape depicted in Figure 4.5, the production function is said to exhibit a *diminishing rate of technical substitution* (RTS), i.e., the isoquants get flatter as x_1 increases. In such a case, (11) will *automatically* be satisfied at any point where (10) holds.)

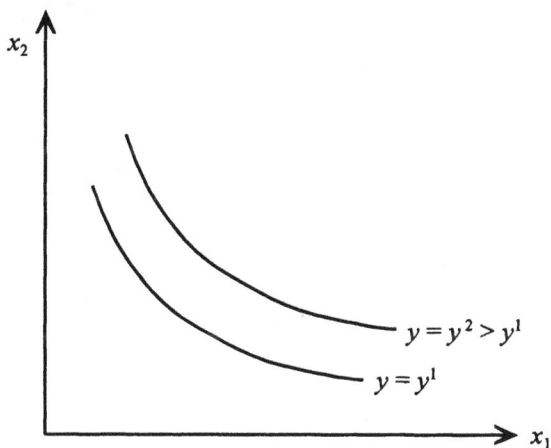

Figure 4.5

Now, define

$$F^1(x_1, x_2, \lambda, \pi) = w_1 - \lambda f_1(x_1, x_2)$$

$$F^2(x_1, x_2, \lambda, \pi) = (\pi w_2^l + (1 - \pi) w_2^H) - \lambda f_2(x_1, x_2)$$

$$F^3(x_1, x_2, \lambda, \pi) = y - f(x_1, x_2).$$

Expected cost is minimized when

$$F^1(x_1, x_2, \lambda, \pi) = 0$$

$$F^2(x_1, x_2, \lambda, \pi) = 0 \qquad\qquad (12)$$

and

$$F^3(x_1, x_2, \lambda, \pi) = 0.$$

We want to solve (12) for the expected cost minimizing input levels and the Lagrange multiplier in terms of the probability parameter π:

$$x_1 = x_1^*(\pi)$$

$$x_2 = x_2^*(\pi)$$

$$\lambda = \lambda^*(\pi).$$

By the Implicit Function Theorem, (12) will define these functions provided that:

$$|J| = \begin{vmatrix} F_1^1 & F_2^1 & F_\lambda^1 \\ F_1^2 & F_2^2 & F_\lambda^2 \\ F_1^3 & F_2^3 & F_\lambda^3 \end{vmatrix} \neq 0.$$

Using the definitions of F^1, F^2, and F^3 we obtain

$$\begin{array}{lll} F_1^1 = -\lambda f_{11} & F_2^1 = -\lambda f_{12} & F_\lambda^1 = -f_1 \\ F_1^2 = -\lambda f_{21} & F_2^2 = -\lambda f_{22} & F_\lambda^2 = -f_2 \\ F_1^3 = -f_1 & F_2^3 = -f_2 & F_\lambda^3 = 0. \end{array}$$

Therefore

$$|J| = \begin{vmatrix} -\lambda f_{11} & -\lambda f_{12} & -f_1 \\ -\lambda f_{21} & -\lambda f_{22} & -f_2 \\ -f_1 & -f_2 & 0 \end{vmatrix} < 0$$

since the second-order condition (11) holds.

Now since $|J| \neq 0$, the Implicit Function Theorem insures that the functions $x_1 = x_1^*(\pi)$, $x_2 = x_2^*(\pi)$, and $\lambda = \lambda^*(\pi)$ exist, are differentiable, and satisfy the identities

$$F^1\Big(x_1^*(\pi),\ x_2^*(\pi),\ \lambda^*(\pi),\ \pi\Big) = w_1 - \lambda^*(\pi) \cdot f_1\Big(x_1^*(\pi),\ x_2^*(\pi)\Big) \equiv 0$$

$$F^2\left(x_1^*(\pi),\ x_2^*(\pi),\ \lambda^*(\pi),\ \pi\right) = \left(\pi w_2^L + (1 - \pi)w_2^H\right)$$
$$- \lambda^*(\pi) \cdot f_2\left(x_1^*(\pi),\ x_2^*(\pi)\right) \equiv 0$$

$$F^3\left(x_1^*(\pi),\ x_2^*(\pi),\ \lambda^*(\pi),\ \pi\right) = y - f\left(x_1^*(\pi),\ x_2^*(\pi)\right) \equiv 0$$

As usual, we obtain the comparative statics derivatives $dx_1^*/d\pi$, $dx_2^*/d\pi$, and $d\lambda^*/d\pi$ by differentiating these identities with respect to π:

$$-\left(\lambda^* \left(f_{11}\frac{dx_1^*}{d\pi} + f_{12}\frac{dx_2^*}{d\pi}\right) + f_1\frac{d\lambda^*}{d\pi}\right) = 0$$

$$\left(w_2^L - w_2^H\right) - \left(\lambda^* \left(f_{21}\frac{dx_1^*}{d\pi} + f_{22}\frac{dx_2^*}{d\pi}\right) + f_2\frac{d\lambda^*}{d\pi}\right) = 0$$

$$-f_1\frac{dx_1^*}{d\pi} - f_2\frac{dx_2^*}{d\pi} = 0.$$

Rearranging, we obtain

$$-\lambda^* f_{11} \cdot \left(\frac{dx_1^*}{d\pi}\right) - \lambda^* f_{12} \cdot \left(\frac{dx_2^*}{d\pi}\right) - f_1 \cdot \left(\frac{d\lambda^*}{d\pi}\right) = 0$$

$$-\lambda^* f_{21} \cdot \left(\frac{dx_1^*}{d\pi}\right) - \lambda^* f_{22} \cdot \left(\frac{dx_2^*}{d\pi}\right) - f_2 \cdot \left(\frac{d\lambda^*}{d\pi}\right) = w_2^H - w_2^L$$

$$-f_1 \cdot \left(\frac{dx_1^*}{d\pi}\right) - f_2 \cdot \left(\frac{dx_2^*}{d\pi}\right) + 0 \cdot \left(\frac{d\lambda^*}{d\pi}\right) = 0.$$

Now, apply Cramer's Rule to obtain the comparative statics derivatives:

$$\frac{dx_1^*}{d\pi} = \frac{\begin{vmatrix} 0 & -\lambda^* f_{12} & -f_1 \\ w_2^H - w_2^L & -\lambda^* f_{22} & -f_2 \\ 0 & -f_2 & 0 \end{vmatrix}}{\begin{vmatrix} -\lambda^* f_{11} & -\lambda^* f_{12} & -f_1 \\ -\lambda^* f_{21} & -\lambda^* f_{22} & -f_2 \\ -f_1 & -f_2 & 0 \end{vmatrix}} = \frac{\left(w_2^H - w_2^L\right) f_1 f_2}{|J|} < 0$$

$$\frac{dx_2^*}{d\pi} = \frac{\begin{vmatrix} -\lambda^* f_{11} & 0 & -f_1 \\ -\lambda^* f_{21} & w_2^H - w_2^L & -f_2 \\ -f_1 & 0 & 0 \end{vmatrix}}{\begin{vmatrix} -\lambda^* f_{11} & -\lambda^* f_{12} & -f_1 \\ -\lambda^* f_{21} & -\lambda^* f_{22} & -f_2 \\ -f_1 & -f_2 & 0 \end{vmatrix}} = \frac{-f_1^2 \cdot \left(w_2^H - w_2^L\right)}{|J|} > 0$$

and

$$\frac{d\lambda^*}{d\pi} = \frac{\begin{vmatrix} -\lambda^* f_{11} & -\lambda^* f_{12} & 0 \\ -\lambda^* f_{21} & -\lambda^* f_{22} & w_2^H - w_2^L \\ -f_1 & -f_2 & 0 \end{vmatrix}}{\begin{vmatrix} -\lambda^* f_{11} & -\lambda^* f_{12} & -f_1 \\ -\lambda^* f_{21} & -\lambda^* f_{22} & -f_2 \\ -f_1 & -f_2 & 0 \end{vmatrix}} = \frac{\lambda^* \left(w_2^H - w_2^L\right) \cdot \left(f_{11} f_2 + f_{12} f_1\right)}{|J|} \begin{array}{c} > \\ = 0 \\ < \end{array}$$

since $|J| < 0$. Thus, an increase in the probability that the price of input two is low will induce the firm to employ more x_2 and less x_1. The sign of $d\lambda^*/d\pi$ is indeterminant without additional assumptions regarding the production function. The model is illustrated in Figure 4.6.

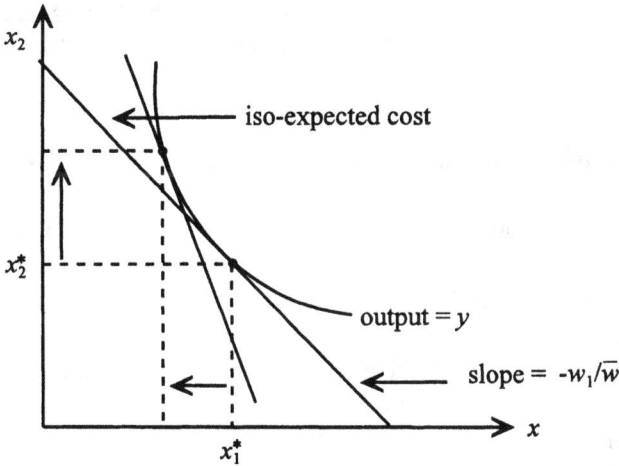

Figure 4.6

The firm wants to produce the output level y in the least-cost way. The iso-expected cost lines are all lines of the form

$$w_1 \cdot x_1 + \left(\pi w_2^L + (1 - \pi)w_2^H\right) \cdot x_2 = \text{constant}.$$

The firm wants to be on the lowest iso-expected cost line that has a point in common with the isoquant for output level y. Combining the first-order conditions $L_1 = 0$ and $L_2 = 0$ and eliminating the multiplier implies that the solution is a tangency point where

$$\text{RTS} = \frac{f_1}{f_2} = \frac{w_1}{\pi w_2^L + (1 - \pi)w_2^H}. \tag{13}$$

Now, if π increases, $\overline{w} = \pi w_2^L + (1 - \pi)w_2^H$ will decrease since $\partial\overline{w}/\partial\pi = w_2^L - w_2^H < 0$. The firm must adjust its input levels so as to continue to satisfy (13) while remaining on the isoquant for y units of output. Since $\overline{w}$ decreases, $w_1/(\pi w_2^L + (1 - \pi)w_2^H)$ increases. Hence the RTS at the new solution must be higher than at the original solution (x_1^*, x_2^*). Therefore, the new expected cost minimization point lies above and to the left of (x_1^*, x_2^*). The firm is substituting the input whose expected cost has fallen for the input whose cost has remained the same.

4.5 Second-Order Conditions and the Implicit Function Theorem

In Chapter 2 we saw that comparative statics derivatives are well defined when the determinant of the appropriate Jacobian matrix is non-zero. In this chapter we have seen that in models based on unconstrained optimization problems, this Jacobian is the determinant of the Hessian matrix of the objective function. In models based on constrained optimization problems, this Jacobian is the bordered Hessian. For any economic model to be meaningful, the second-order condition(s) must be assumed to hold (as in Application 4.3) or there must be sufficient structure imposed on the model so that the second-order conditions are implied by the model (such as Application 4.4). In any case, we observe that it is not necessary to repeatedly check that the hypothesis of the Implicit Function Theorem (i.e., the non-zero Jacobian determinant) is satisfied. The applicability of the Implicit Function Theorem will automatically be insured by the satisfaction of the second-order conditions in any optimization-based model.

Problems

1. (Hands, 1991) When an excise tax of $\$t$ per unit sold is levied on a commodity, the price that consumers pay (p) equals the amount received by the sellers (c) plus the tax: $p = c + t$. Market equilibrium then requires $D(p) = S(c)$ where $D(\cdot)$ and $S(\cdot)$ denote the market demand and supply functions, which are assumed to satisfy $D' < 0$ and $S' > 0$. Let p^* denote the equilibrium price, with $c^* = p^* - t$.

   a. Compute the comparative statics derivatives
   $$\frac{dp^*}{dt} \quad \text{and} \quad \frac{dc^*}{dt}$$
   and determine their signs.

   b. What happens to the equilibrium quantity x^* when t increases?

   c. Illustrate graphically in a supply/demand diagram showing p^* and c^*.

2. Consider a firm with profit function $\pi = pAf(x) - wx$ where f is the production function, x is the input level, A denotes a technological parameter, and p and w are output and input prices, respectively. Let x^* maximize profit. Compute
   $$\frac{dx^*}{dA}$$
   and show that the result derived in Application 3.2 is a special case of this formula.

3. A public good produced in quantity x provides benefit $B(x)$ to each of n-consumers. Assume $B' > 0$ and $B'' < 0$. The cost of providing each unit of x is $c > 0$. Net social benefit is $NSB = nB(x) - cx$. A policy maker wants to choose x to maximize NSB. Show that
   $$\frac{dx^*}{dn} > 0 \quad \text{and} \quad \frac{dx^*}{dc} < 0.$$
   where x^* maximizes NSB.

4. (Hands, 1991) A monopolist produces output y and has an advertising expenditure of A. Profit is $\pi = R(y, A) - c(y) - A$ where $R(\cdot)$ is the revenue function and $c(\cdot)$ is the cost function. Assume $R_{yA} > 0$.

   a. Explain the meaning of $R_{yA} > 0$.
   b. Suppose that in the short-run, A is fixed and therefore enters the profit function as a parameter. Let y^* maximize profit. Compute

   $$\frac{dy^*}{dA}.$$

   Is its sign determinant?

5. (Varian, 1992) Consider a monopolist that produces output y and has cost function

   $$C(y) = cy \quad c > 0$$

   and faces demand curve

   $$p = p(y, t)$$

   where t is a parameter that shifts the demand curve. Let y^* denote the profit maximizing output level.

   a. Compute $\dfrac{dy^*}{dt}$. Is its sign determinant?
   b. How is the comparative statics derivative affected if the demand curve is of the form $p = a(y) + b(t)$?

6. Consider the tire manufacturer discussed in Application 3.4. Assume only that the cost function is $C(x_1, x_2)$. Compute

   $$\frac{dx_1^*}{dT} \quad \text{and} \quad \frac{dx_2^*}{dT}$$

   and show that the results in the text are special cases of these formulas.

7. Consider a monopoly that produces its output y in two separate plants. The cost functions are

$c_1(y_1)$	Plant 1
$c_2(y_2) = cy_2$	Plant 2

   where $c_1' > 0$, $c_1'' > 0$, and $c > 0$. Total output is $y = y_1 + y_2$. The firm desires to minimize the total cost of producing output level y.

   a. Characterize the optimal allocation of production between plants.
   b. How is the optimal allocation affected by an increase in y?
   c. Why is all the additional production allocated to Plant 2?
   d. Illustrate graphically in the manner of Application 3.3.

8. (Hands, 1991) A profit maximizing, perfectly competitive firm produces output y from inputs x_1 and x_2 according to the *additively separable* production function

   $$y = f(x_1) + g(x_2).$$

   Output price is p and input prices are w_1 and w_2. Show that the comparative statics derivatives satisfy

   $$\frac{\partial x_1^*}{\partial p} = -f' \cdot \left(\frac{\partial x_1^*}{\partial w_1} \right)$$

   and

   $$\frac{\partial x_2^*}{\partial p} = -g' \cdot \left(\frac{\partial x_2^*}{\partial w_2} \right).$$

9. Consider a perfectly competitive industry where *each* firm has the marginal cost function $MC(y)$. Total market demand for the output y is $D(p)$ where p denotes market price. There are n-firms in the market. A market equilibrium may be characterized by

$$p = MC(y)$$
$$ny = D(p).$$

The first condition insures that each firm is maximizing profit and the second insures that total market output equals demand (i.e., market clearance). Assume that $MC' > 0$ and $D' < 0$. Let p^* denote the equilibrium price, y^* denote the individual firm's profit maximizing output level, and $Y^* \equiv ny^*$ denote total market output. Compute:

$$\frac{dp^*}{dn} \qquad \frac{dy^*}{dn} \qquad \text{and} \qquad \frac{dY^*}{dn}$$

and determine their signs.

10. A firm is called a *natural monopoly* if its technology exhibits economies of scale (i.e., decreasing average cost) over the entire range of output levels. Consider a regulated natural monopoly with average cost function

$$AC(w, y)$$

where y denotes output and w denotes the input price. Assume $AC_y < 0$ and $AC_w > 0$. The firm faces the demand curve

$$D(p, M)$$

where p denotes the price of the monopoly output and M denotes consumer income. Assume $D_p < 0$ and $D_M > 0$. An *average cost pricing equilibrium* (*ACPE*) is a pair (p, y) satisfying

$$p = AC(w, y)$$

and

$$y = D(p, M).$$

The first condition insures that the firm earns zero profit, and the second insures that total market demand is satisfied. Let (p^*, y^*) denote the solution.

a. Assume that
$$\frac{1}{D_p} < AC.$$

This insures that the demand curve is more steeply sloped than the average cost curve. Perform a comparative statics analysis of the impact of changes in w and M on p^* and y^*.

b. Illustrate graphically, showing D and AC.

5. Comparative Statics Theorems for Parameterized Optimization Problems

5.1. Introduction

In the preceding chapters, we have considered optimization problems in which the objective functions and/or the constraints have depended functionally on one or more parameters. These are referred to as *parameterized optimization problems*. In this chapter, we present a series of important theorems regarding the comparative statics properties of both constrained and unconstrained parameterized optimization problems.

In order to introduce some of the concepts involved in these theorems, consider the maximization problem (P):

(P)   Maximize $F(x, a)$
        x

where F is C^2, a is a parameter, and $F_{xa} \neq 0$. The first-order necessary condition for a (local) maximum of F is $F_x = 0$, and the second-order sufficient condition requires $F_{xx} < 0$ at the point where $F_x = 0$.

Now, let $x = x^*(a)$ denote the solution. The comparative statics derivative dx^*/da is obtained by differentiating the identity

$$F_x\left(x^*(a), a\right) \equiv 0$$

with respect to a, yielding

$$\frac{dx^*}{da} = \frac{-F_{xa}}{F_{xx}}.$$

Multiplying both sides by F_{xa}, one obtains

$$\frac{dx^*}{da} \cdot F_{xa} = \frac{-F_{xa} \cdot F_{xa}}{F_{xx}} = \frac{-\left(F_{xa}\right)^2}{F_{xx}}.$$

Now $F_{xx} < 0$ by the second-order condition and $\left(F_{xa}\right)^2 > 0$, implying that

$$\frac{dx^*}{da} \cdot F_{xa} > 0.$$

Hence, we conclude that

$$\text{sign } \frac{dx^*}{da} = \text{sign } F_{xa},$$

i.e., $F_{xa} > 0$ implies $dx^*/da > 0$ and $F_{xa} < 0$ implies $dx^*/da < 0$. This is a simple illustration of the *Conjugate Pairs Theorem*, which tells us, in this case, that the sign of the comparative statics derivative is completely determined by the sign of the second-order cross partial F_{xa}. We shall see repeatedly how the signs of various cross partials play a critical role in determining the comparative statics properties of optimization-based models. This fact is actually quite elementary and can be illustrated by the following graphical argument.

Suppose, for example, that $F_{xa} < 0$. The Conjugate Pairs Theorem implies that the comparative statics derivative dx^*/da must be negative. Consider now Figure 5.1

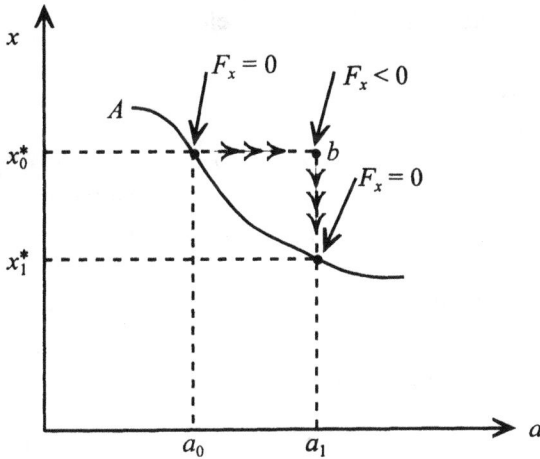

Figure 5.1

Suppose that when $a = a_0$, $x = x_0^*$ solves problem (P). Then $F_x(x_0^*, a_0) = 0$. We want to show that the (differentiable) function $x = x^*(a)$ must have negative slope. To this end, consider another value of $a = a_1 > a_0$. Let x_1^* denote the corresponding solution. Then it is sufficient to show that $x_1^* < x_0^*$ since this will imply that the function $x = x^*(a)$ (whose graph we denote by A) appears as depicted in Figure 5.1

We know that $F_x = 0$ at (x_0^*, a_0). Consider now moving to the right from (x_0^*, a_0) toward point b. It must be the case that $F_x < 0$ at point b. This is true because with $F_{xa} < 0$, an increase in a must decrease F_x. Now, starting at b, to return to A we must change x in such a way as to make $F_x(x, a_1) = 0$. Since $F_{xx} < 0$, we know that decreasing x will increase F_x. Hence the point (x_1^*, a_1) must lie directly below point b. Thus, since $a_1 > a_0$ and $x_1^* < x_0^*$, we have

$$\frac{\Delta x^*}{\Delta a} < 0$$

and the claim is proven. Observe also that the comparative statics derivative dx^*/da is simply the slope of A at any particular point. (Note: Since the assumptions that $F_{xa} < 0$ and $F_{xx} < 0$ are purely local in nature, the distances $(x_0^* - x_1^*)$ and $(a_1 - a_0)$ in Figure 5.1 should be regarded as very small.)

Again consider problem (P), letting $x = x^*(a)$ denote the solution. This solution may be substituted back into F, yielding

$$V(a) \equiv F\left(x^*(a), a\right).$$

The function $V(a)$ is called the *Value Function* or the *Indirect Objective Function*. It tells us the *maximum* value of F for each a. It must be stressed that the value function arises from (or is based on) an optimization problem and does not exist independent of it.

Now, differentiate the value function with respect to a:

$$V'(a) = F_x \cdot \frac{dx^*}{da} + F_a.$$

Since F is maximized for each a, we have $F_x = 0$ from the first-order condition. Hence

$$V'(a) = F_a.$$

This result is called the *Envelope Theorem* and, despite its deceptively simple appearance, is profound. It tells us that the derivative of the value function with respect to the parameter a is equal to the partial derivative of F with respect to that parameter *when the derivative is evaluated at the optimal point* .

The logic of the Envelope Theorem may be appreciated by considering the following *channel map*.

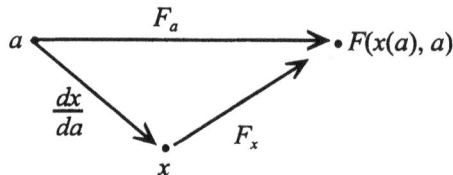

Figure 5.2

When a changes, there are two effects. The change in a directly affects F, i.e., F_a, and the change in a affects x, which in turn affects F, i.e., $(dx/da) \cdot F_x$. However, since $x = x^*$ is optimal, $F_x = 0$ and the lower channel of Figure 5.2 vanishes, leaving only the direct effect. Figure 5.3 provides an illustration.

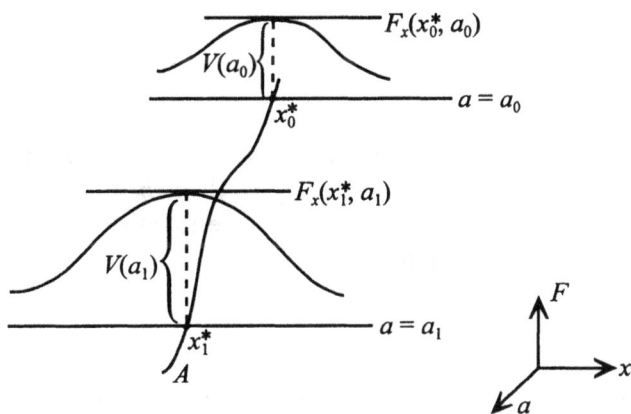

Figure 5.3

The axes in the lower right show the orientation of the diagram. As in Figure 5.1, the curve labeled A is $x = x^*(a)$. For each value of a (a_0 and a_1) the value function gives the maximum value of F. Therefore, $V = F|_A$, the restriction of F to the curve A. The Envelope Theorem tells us that its derivative may be obtained simply by computing F_a.

Application 5.1

Return to Application 3.2 where A denotes the state of technology and the firm's profit is $\pi(x) = 2Ax^{\frac{1}{2}} - x$. We have shown that the profit maximizing input level is $x^*(A) = A^2$ and that the comparative statics derivative is $dx^*/dA = 2A > 0$.

The Conjugate Pairs Theorem and the Envelope Theorem tell us a great deal about the comparative statics properties of the model *without even computing x^* and dx^*/dA*. Specifically, the Conjugate Pairs Theorem tells us that the sign of dx^*/dA must equal the sign of $\pi_{xA} = 1/x^{\frac{1}{2}} > 0$. Hence, a technological improvement must result in the firm using more x. In addition, the value function is a function of the parameter in the model: $V = V(A)$.

By the Envelope Theorem,

$$V'(A) = \frac{d\pi}{dA} = 2x^{\frac{1}{2}} > 0.$$

In this case, the value function tells us the *maximum* level of profit attainable for each level of technology. Since $d\pi/dA > 0$, we know that an improvement in technology will increase the profit earned by the firm *when x is chosen optimally*.

To confirm this, we may compute the value function explicitly by substituting the solution $x^*(A) = A^2$ into $\pi(x)$ yielding

$$\pi^* \big(\equiv V(A) \big) = 2A(x^*)^{\frac{1}{2}} - x^* = A^2.$$

We observe that $d\pi^*/dA = 2A = 2(x^*)^{\frac{1}{2}} > 0$ as claimed above.

5.2. Conjugate Pairs Theorems

In this and subsequent sections, we shall denote the parameters in the models by a, b, and c. We assume that all functions are C^2 and that the relevant second-order conditions hold for each maximization problem. We shall also employ an important theorem from calculus called *Young's Theorem*, which says that for a C^2 function, the second-order cross partials are equal. For example, for a function of two variables $f(x_1, x_2)$, Young's Theorem states that if f is C^2, then $f_{12} = f_{21}$. The result generalizes to C^2 functions of any number of variables, implying that $f_{ij} = f_{ji}$, $i \neq j$. Careful inspection of the Hessians and Bordered Hessians in the applications in Chapters 3 and 4 confirm this. Because of Young's Theorem, these matrices are said to be *symmetric*.

Theorem 5-1A

Consider an unconstrained maximization problem for which the first-order necessary conditions are of the form

$F_x(x, y, a) = 0$

$F_y(x, y, b) = 0.$

Let $\left(x^*(a, b),\ y^*(a, b)\right)$ denote the solution. Then

$$F_{xa} \cdot \frac{\partial x^*}{\partial a} > 0 \qquad \text{and} \qquad F_{yb} \cdot \frac{\partial y^*}{\partial b} > 0.$$

Proof: As we have seen, the solutions satisfy the first-order necessary condition as identities

$$F_x\left(x^*(a, b),\ y^*(a, b),\ a\right) \equiv 0$$

$$F_y\left(x^*(a, b),\ y^*(a, b),\ b\right) \equiv 0.$$

Differentiation with respect to the parameters, solving via Cramer's Rule and invoking the second-order condition establishes the results. The details are left as an exercise.

Theorem 5-1B

Consider a constrained maximization problem for which the first-order necessary conditions are of the form

$L_x(x, y, \lambda, a) = 0$

$L_y(x, y, \lambda, b) = 0$

$(L_\lambda =)\ g(x, y, c) = 0$

where L denotes the Lagrangian function and λ the corresponding multiplier. Let $\left(x^*(a, b, c),\ y^*(a, b, c),\ \lambda^*(a, b, c)\right)$ denote the solution. Then

$$L_{xa} \cdot \frac{\partial x^*}{\partial a} > 0 \qquad \text{and} \qquad L_{yb} \cdot \frac{\partial y^*}{\partial b} > 0.$$

(For a minimization problem, the inequalities are reversed.)

Proof: The solutions satisfy

$$L_x\left(x^*(a, b, c), y^*(a, b, c), \lambda^*(a, b, c), a\right) \equiv 0$$

$$L_y\left(x^*(a, b, c), y^*(a, b, c), \lambda^*(a, b, c), b\right) \equiv 0$$

$$(L_\lambda =) \, g\left(x^*(a, b, c), y^*(a, b, c), c\right) \equiv 0.$$

To show that

$$L_{xa} \cdot \frac{\partial x^*}{\partial a} > 0$$

differentiate with respect to a:

$$L_{xx}\left(\frac{\partial x^*}{\partial a}\right) + L_{xy}\left(\frac{\partial y^*}{\partial a}\right) + L_{x\lambda}\left(\frac{\partial \lambda^*}{\partial a}\right) + L_{xa} = 0$$

$$L_{yx}\left(\frac{\partial x^*}{\partial a}\right) + L_{yy}\left(\frac{\partial y^*}{\partial a}\right) + L_{y\lambda}\left(\frac{\partial \lambda^*}{\partial a}\right) = 0$$

$$g_x\left(\frac{\partial x^*}{\partial a}\right) + g_y\left(\frac{\partial y^*}{\partial a}\right) + 0\left(\frac{\partial \lambda^*}{\partial a}\right) = 0.$$

Now use the fact that $L_{x\lambda} = L_{\lambda x} = g_x$, $L_{y\lambda} = L_{\lambda y} = g_y$ and Cramer's Rule to obtain

$$\frac{\partial x^*}{\partial a} = \frac{\begin{vmatrix} -L_{xa} & L_{xy} & g_x \\ 0 & L_{yy} & g_y \\ 0 & g_y & 0 \\ L_{xx} & L_{xy} & g_x \\ L_{yx} & L_{yy} & g_y \\ g_x & g_y & 0 \end{vmatrix}}{\begin{vmatrix} L_{xx} & L_{xy} & g_x \\ L_{yx} & L_{yy} & g_y \\ g_x & g_y & 0 \end{vmatrix}} = \frac{L_{xa}\left(g_y\right)^2}{|J|},$$

which implies that

$$\frac{\partial x^*}{\partial a} \cdot L_{xa} = \frac{\left(L_{xa}\right)^2 \cdot \left(g_y\right)^2}{|J|} > 0$$

since $|J| > 0$ as a consequence of the second-order condition. The same applies to $\partial y^*/\partial b$. For a minimization problem, $|J| < 0$ and the inequalities reverse.

5.3. Envelope Theorems

Theorem 5-2A

Consider finding an unconstrained maximum of $F(x, y, a, b)$. Let $V(a, b)$ be the corresponding value function. Then

$V_a = F_a$ and $V_b = F_b$.

Proof: The value function is

$$V(a, b) \equiv F\left(x^*(a, b), y^*(a, b), a, b\right)$$

where $\left(x^*(a, b), y^*(a, b)\right)$ denotes the solution. Now differentiate with respect to the parameters and invoke the first-order necessary conditions for a maximum. The details are left as an exercise.

Theorem 5-2B

Consider the constrained maximization problem:

Maximize $f(x, y, a, b)$ subject to $g(x, y, a, b) = 0$.
$\quad x, y$

Let L denote the associated Lagrangian function and let $V(a, b)$ denote the value function. Then

$V_a = L_a$ and $V_b = L_b$.

   Proof: Let $L = f(x, y, a, b) + \lambda g(x, y, a, b)$. The solution to the problem $\left(x^*(a, b), y^*(a, b), \lambda^*(a, b)\right)$ satisfies the first-order necessary conditions

$L_x\left(x^*(a, b), y^*(a, b), \lambda^*(a, b), a, b\right) \equiv 0$

$L_y\left(x^*(a, b), y^*(a, b), \lambda^*(a, b), a, b\right) \equiv 0$

and

$g\left(x^*(a, b), y^*(a, b), a, b\right) \equiv 0$.   (1)

The value function is $V(a, b) \equiv f\left(x^*(a, b), y^*(a, b), a, b\right)$. Differentiation with respect to a yields

$$V_a = f_x \frac{\partial x^*}{\partial a} + f_y \frac{\partial y^*}{\partial a} + f_a.$$

Now, differentiate (1) with respect to a to obtain

$$g_x \frac{\partial x^*}{\partial a} + g_y \frac{\partial y^*}{\partial a} + g_a = 0.$$

Multiplying this expression by λ^* yields

$$\lambda^* g_x \frac{\partial x^*}{\partial a} + \lambda^* g_y \frac{\partial y^*}{\partial a} + \lambda^* g_a = \lambda^* \cdot (0) = 0.$$

Now

$$V_a = f_x \frac{\partial x^*}{\partial a} + f_y \frac{\partial y^*}{\partial a} + f_a$$

$$= f_x \frac{\partial x^*}{\partial a} + f_y \frac{\partial y^*}{\partial a} + f_a + 0$$

$$= f_x \frac{\partial x^*}{\partial a} + f_y \frac{\partial y^*}{\partial a} + f_a + \lambda^* g_x \frac{\partial x^*}{\partial a} + \lambda^* g_y \frac{\partial y^*}{\partial a} + \lambda^* g_a$$

$$= \left(f_x + \lambda^* g_x \right) \frac{\partial x^*}{\partial a} + \left(f_y + \lambda^* g_y \right) \frac{\partial y^*}{\partial a} + \left(f_a + \lambda^* g_a \right)$$

$$= L_x \frac{\partial x^*}{\partial a} + L_y \frac{\partial y^*}{\partial a} + L_a = L_a$$

since $L_x = L_y = 0$ by the first-order necessary conditions. The same applies to parameter b.

One extremely important implication of Theorem 5-2B arises within the context of the following problem.

Maximize $f(x, y)$ subject to $h(x, y) = k$

where k is a parameter. Define $g(x, y, k) \equiv k - h(x, y)$ and let $V(k)$ denote the value function. Here the Lagrangian function is

$$L(x, y, \lambda, k) = f(x, y) + \lambda\big(k - h(x, y)\big).$$

Let $x = x^*(k)$, $y = y^*(k)$, and $\lambda = \lambda^*(k)$ denote the solution. Applying Theorem 5-2B, we obtain

$$V'(k) = L_k = \lambda = \lambda^*(k).$$

This tells us that for this maximization problem, the solution value of the Lagrange multiplier equals the rate of change of the *maximum* value of the objective function with respect to changes in k, the value of the constraint. In many economic applications, k denotes the stock of a resource and f denotes profit, utility, or output. Since $dV/dk = \lambda^*$, $\lambda^* \Delta k \approx \Delta V$, the (approximate) increase in profit, utility, or output that can be obtained if $\Delta k > 0$ additional units of the resource become available. λ^* is called the *shadow price* of the resource and reflects its marginal value. We shall investigate one important application of this concept in Section 5.5.

5.4. Reciprocity Theorems

Theorem 5-3A

Consider an unconstrained maximization problem for which the first-order necessary conditions are of the form

$$F_x(x, y, a) = 0$$

$$F_y(x, y, b) = 0.$$

Let $\left(x^*(a, b), y^*(a, b)\right)$ denote the solution. Then

$$F_{xa} \cdot \frac{\partial x^*}{\partial b} = F_{yb} \cdot \frac{\partial y^*}{\partial a}.$$

Proof: The proof is left as an exercise.

Theorem 5-3B

Consider a constrained maximization problem for which the first-order necessary conditions are of the form

$$L_x(x, y, \lambda, a) = 0$$

$$L_y(x, y, \lambda, b) = 0$$

$$(L_\lambda =) \, g(x, y, c) = 0$$

where L denotes the Lagrangian function and λ the corresponding multiplier. Let $\left(x^*(a, b, c), \, y^*(a, b, c), \, \lambda^*(a, b, c)\right)$ denote the solution. Then

$$L_{xa} \frac{\partial x^*}{\partial c} = g_c \frac{\partial \lambda^*}{\partial a} \qquad , \qquad L_{yb} \frac{\partial y^*}{\partial c} = g_c \frac{\partial \lambda^*}{\partial b}$$

and

$$L_{xa} \frac{\partial x^*}{\partial b} = L_{yb} \frac{\partial y^*}{\partial a}.$$

Proof: For brevity, we prove only the first result. The remaining results are obtained in the same manner. We need to compute $\partial x^*/\partial c$ and $\partial \lambda^*/\partial a$. We shall use $|J|$ to denote the same determinant as in the proof of Theorem 5-1B.

Differentiating the first-order conditions with respect to a yields

$$L_{xx}\left(\frac{\partial x^*}{\partial a}\right) + L_{xy}\left(\frac{\partial y^*}{\partial a}\right) + L_{x\lambda}\left(\frac{\partial \lambda^*}{\partial a}\right) + L_{xa} = 0$$

$$L_{yx}\left(\frac{\partial x^*}{\partial a}\right) + L_{yy}\left(\frac{\partial y^*}{\partial a}\right) + L_{y\lambda}\left(\frac{\partial \lambda^*}{\partial a}\right) = 0$$

$$g_x\left(\frac{\partial x^*}{\partial a}\right) + g_y\left(\frac{\partial y^*}{\partial a}\right) = 0.$$

Use $L_{\lambda x} = L_{x\lambda} = g_x$, $L_{\lambda y} = L_{y\lambda} = g_y$ and Cramer's Rule to obtain

$$\frac{\partial \lambda^*}{\partial a} = \frac{\begin{vmatrix} L_{xx} & L_{xy} & -L_{xa} \\ L_{yx} & L_{yy} & 0 \\ g_x & g_y & 0 \end{vmatrix}}{|J|} = \frac{L_{xa}g_xL_{yy} - L_{xa}L_{yx}g_y}{|J|}.$$

Now, to obtain $\partial x^*/\partial c$, differentiate the first-order conditions with respect to c:

$$L_{xx}\left(\frac{\partial x^*}{\partial c}\right) + L_{xy}\left(\frac{\partial y^*}{\partial c}\right) + L_{x\lambda}\left(\frac{\partial \lambda^*}{\partial c}\right) = 0$$

$$L_{yx}\left(\frac{\partial x^*}{\partial c}\right) + L_{yy}\left(\frac{\partial y^*}{\partial c}\right) + L_{y\lambda}\left(\frac{\partial \lambda^*}{\partial c}\right) = 0$$

$$g_x\left(\frac{\partial x^*}{\partial c}\right) + g_y\left(\frac{\partial y^*}{\partial c}\right) + g_c = 0.$$

Hence,

$$\frac{\partial x^*}{\partial c} = \frac{\begin{vmatrix} 0 & L_{xy} & g_x \\ 0 & L_{yy} & g_y \\ -g_c & g_y & 0 \end{vmatrix}}{|J|} = \frac{L_{yy}g_xg_c - L_{xy}g_yg_c}{|J|}.$$

Therefore

$$L_{xa}\frac{\partial x^*}{\partial c} = \frac{L_{xa}L_{yy}g_xg_c - L_{xa}L_{xy}g_yg_c}{|J|}.$$

and

$$g_c \frac{\partial \lambda^*}{\partial a} = \frac{g_c L_{xa} g_x L_{yy} - g_c L_{xa} L_{yx} g_y}{|J|}.$$

The result follows since $L_{xy} = L_{yx}$.

We conclude this section with several comments. First, we have used the fact that $L_{xy} = L_{yx}$ in the proof of Theorem 5-3B. The proof of Theorem 5-3A employs the fact tha $F_{xy} = F_{yx}$. Indeed, it is a general truth that all reciprocity theorems are a direct consequence of Young's Theorem. Second, as regards Theorem 5-3, it should be stressed that the maximization hypothesis implies a *symmetry* condition on a subset of the comparative statics derivatives, not (necessarily) a sign. Third, as stated, the maximization problems we have considered are quite general. As we shall see in Section 5.5, the economic structure imposed on optimization models will often reduce the complexity of the comparative statics properties of the models. In addition, this structure greatly increases the ability of the comparative statics methodology to yield testable hypotheses, i.e., to lead to *definitive* sign predictions on the comparative statics derivatives. Finally, we shall see that appropriate application of the Envelope Theorem and Young's Theorem leads to useful conjugate pair and reciprocity results with minimal computation.

5.5. Applications

Application 5.2

Consider a profit maximizing firm that produces output y from input x according to the C^2 production function $y = f(x)$ where $f' > 0$ and $f'' < 0$. The price of output is $p > 0$ and the price of the input is $w > 0$. The firm's objective is to maximize profit $\pi(x, y) = py - wx$ but must satisfy its production constraint. We therefore consider the following constrained maximization problem.

Maximize $py - wx$ subject to $y = f(x)$.
   x, y

We shall examine how the solution to this problem is affected by changes in the parameters p and w.
      Form the Lagrangian function

$$L(x, y, \lambda) = py - wx + \lambda [y - f(x)].$$

The first-order necessary conditions for a constrained profit maximum are

$$L_x = -w - \lambda f'(x) = 0$$

$$L_y = p + \lambda = 0$$

$$L_\lambda = y - f(x) = 0.$$

Now let $g(x, y) = y - f(x)$ and form the bordered Hessian

$$H = \begin{bmatrix} L_{xx} & L_{xy} & g_x \\ L_{yx} & L_{yy} & g_y \\ g_x & g_y & 0 \end{bmatrix} = \begin{bmatrix} -\lambda f'' & 0 & -f' \\ 0 & 0 & 1 \\ -f' & 1 & 0 \end{bmatrix}.$$

Now $|H| = \lambda f'' > 0$ since $f'' < 0$ and $\lambda = -p < 0$ from the first-order conditions. Hence we see that the assumption of diminishing marginal returns (i.e., $f'' < 0$) insures that the point where the first-order conditions hold is in fact a maximum.
      Solving $L_y = 0$ for λ and substituting into $L_x = 0$ yields

$$\frac{w}{p} = f'(x).$$

This condition, along with $L_\lambda = y - f(x) = 0$ characterizes the solution: Moving along the production function, optimality requires that the firm produce where the marginal product of the input equals the price ratio. The situation is illustrated in Figure 5.4.

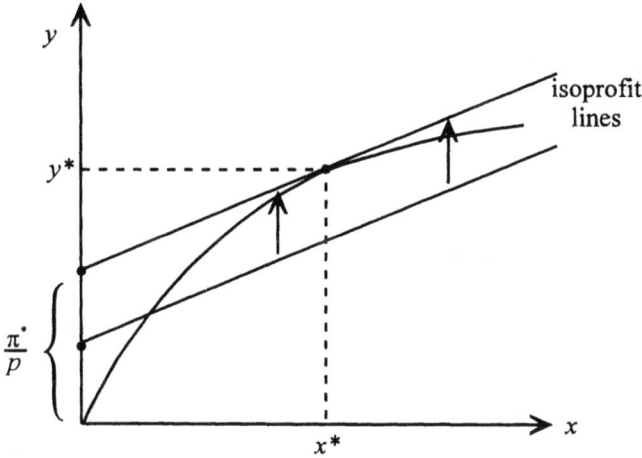

Figure 5.4

The production function has the *concave* shape since $f' > 0$ and $f'' < 0$. The firm's profit is $\pi = py - wx$. The isoprofit lines are all lines of the form $py - wx = \text{constant}$. The firm wants to be on the highest isoprofit line that has a point in common with the production function. The isoprofit lines have slope equal to w/p. At the solution, the slope of the production function must equal the slope of the isoprofit line, i.e., $w/p = f'$. Let (x^*, y^*) denote the solution. Since $\pi = py - wx$, the profit at the optimum is $\pi^* \equiv py^* - wx^*$. The isoprofit line through (x^*, y^*) is $py - wx = \pi^*$, which has y-intercept equal to π^*/p.

The solution values of x, y, and λ are differentiable functions of the parameters:

$$x = x^*(p, w), \quad y = y^*(p, w), \quad \lambda = \lambda^*(p, w).$$

We shall investigate four comparative statics derivatives:

$$\frac{\partial x^*}{\partial p}, \frac{\partial x^*}{\partial w}, \frac{\partial y^*}{\partial p}, \text{ and } \frac{\partial y^*}{\partial w}.$$

The solutions satisfy

$$-w - \lambda^*(p,w) \cdot f'\big(x^*(p,w)\big) \equiv 0$$

$$p + \lambda^*(p,w) \equiv 0$$

$$y^*(p,w) - f\big(x^*(p,w)\big) \equiv 0.$$

Differentiation with respect to p yields

$$-\lambda^* f'' \cdot \left(\frac{\partial x^*}{\partial p}\right) - f' \cdot \left(\frac{\partial \lambda^*}{\partial p}\right) = 0$$

$$1 + \left(\frac{\partial \lambda^*}{\partial p}\right) = 0$$

$$\left(\frac{\partial y^*}{\partial p}\right) - f' \cdot \left(\frac{\partial x^*}{\partial p}\right) = 0.$$

Solving via Cramer's Rule, we obtain

$$\frac{\partial x^*}{\partial p} = \frac{f'}{\lambda^* f''} > 0 \qquad \text{and} \qquad \frac{\partial y^*}{\partial p} = \frac{(f')^2}{\lambda^* f''} > 0.$$

Hence an increase in p will increase output and the associated input level. In addition, an increase in w will decrease output and the associated input level. These facts can be seen by again considering Figure 5.4. An increase in p makes the isoprofit lines flatter and the tangency point must move upward and to the right from (x^*, y^*). An increase in w makes the isoprofit lines steeper and the tangency point must move downward and to the left.

We now consider the implications of the theorems for this problem. The Conjugate Pairs Theorem states that

$$L_{xw} \cdot \frac{\partial x^*}{\partial w} > 0 \quad \text{and} \quad L_{yp} \cdot \frac{\partial y^*}{\partial p} > 0.$$

Since $L_{xw} = -1$, we have $\partial x^*/\partial w < 0$. In addition, since $L_{yp} = 1$, $\partial y^*/\partial p > 0$ as we have shown.

Since there is no parameter in the constraint, the only reciprocity condition is the third equality in Theorem 5-3B. In this case, it becomes

$$L_{xw} \cdot \frac{\partial x^*}{\partial p} = L_{yp} \cdot \frac{\partial y^*}{\partial w}.$$

Since $L_{xw} = -1$ and $L_{yp} = 1$, we have

$$-\frac{\partial x^*}{\partial p} = \frac{\partial y^*}{\partial w},$$

which can be confirmed by explicit computation.

Finally, consider the implications of the Envelope Theorem. The value function for this problem is

$$\pi^* \left(\equiv V(p, w) \right) \equiv p \cdot y^* (p, w) - w \cdot x^* (p, w).$$

The Envelope Theorem tells us that since

$$L = py - wx + \lambda [y - f(x)],$$

we have

$$\pi_p^* = y = y^*(p, w) \quad \text{and} \quad \pi_w^* = -x = -x^*(p, w).$$

Hence, the two first-order partial derivatives of the value function (the indirect profit function) are simply the firm's output supply function and (the negative of) the input demand function. (In microeconomic theory, this fact is known as *Hotelling's Lemma*.) Moreover, by Young's Theorem, we know that

$$\pi^*_{pw} = \pi^*_{wp},$$

which implies that

$$\frac{\partial y^*}{\partial w} = -\frac{\partial x^*}{\partial p},$$

which is precisely the reciprocity result obtained earlier.

In the next application, we shall make use of the following fact. Consider a *profit maximizing* firm producing output y from inputs x_1 and x_2 with C^2 production $y = f(x_1, x_2)$. Let (x_1^*, x_2^*) denote the profit maximizing input levels. If the second-order sufficient conditions for a maximum hold, then $f_{11}f_{22} - f_{12}f_{21} > 0$ at (x_1^*, x_2^*).

Application 5.3

Consider a firm that produces output y from inputs x_1 and x_2 with C^2 production function $y = f(x_1, x_2)$. Input prices are (w_1, w_2). Given any output level y, the firm desires to produce it in the least cost manner. Thus, the firm solves

Minimize $w_1x_1 + w_2x_2$ subject to $y = f(x_1, x_2)$.
x_1, x_2

The firm's problem is illustrated in Figure 5.5.

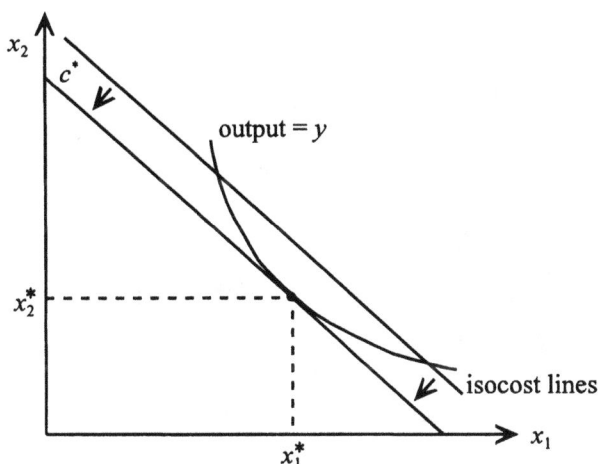

Figure 5.5

The firm's isocost lines are all lines of the form $w_1x_1 + w_2x_2 = $ constant. The firm wants to find the point on the isoquant for y units of output that lies on the lowest possible isocost line. The solution is a tangency point where the slope of the isoquant equals the slope of the isocost line. The solution is the point (x_1^*, x_2^*) in the diagram.

Now consider the firm's constrained minimization problem. Note that y *enters this problem as a parameter.* No particular level of *output* is considered optimal here. We are simply asking *if* the firm wants to produce y units of output, what input combination would do so at least cost? Hence the variables in this model are x_1 and x_2, and the parameters are w_1, w_2 and y.

To analyze the firm's cost minimization problem, form the Lagrangian function

$$L = w_1x_1 + w_2x_2 + \lambda\,[y - f(x_1, x_2)].$$

The first-order necessary conditions for a constrained cost minimum are

$$L_1 = w_1 - \lambda f_1(x_1, x_2) = 0$$

$L_2 = w_2 - \lambda f_2(x_1, x_2) = 0$

$L_\lambda = y - f(x_1, x_2) = 0.$

Now let $g(x_1, x_2, y) = y - f(x_1, x_2)$ and form the bordered Hessian

$$H = \begin{bmatrix} L_{11} & L_{12} & g_1 \\ L_{21} & L_{22} & g_2 \\ g_1 & g_2 & 0 \end{bmatrix} = \begin{bmatrix} -\lambda f_{11} & -\lambda f_{12} & -f_1 \\ -\lambda f_{21} & -\lambda f_{22} & -f_2 \\ -f_1 & -f_2 & 0 \end{bmatrix}.$$

The second-order sufficient condition for a constrained cost minimum requires $|H| < 0$, which is assumed to hold.

Combining the conditions $L_1 = 0$ and $L_2 = 0$ implies

$$\frac{f_1}{f_2} = \text{RTS} = \frac{w_1}{w_2}$$

where the rate of technical substitution (RTS) is the (negative of the) slope of the isoquant. The condition $L_\lambda = 0$ insures that the firm is indeed operating on the isoquant for y units of output.

The solution values of x_1, x_2, and λ are differentiable functions of the parameters:

$x_1 = x_1^*(w_1, w_2\, y), x_2 = x_2^*(w_1, w_2, y), \lambda = \lambda^*(w_1, w_2, y).$

x_1^* and x_2^* are called the *conditional factor (input) demands* since they are conditional upon (i.e., depend upon) the output level.

The value function for the cost minimization problem is

$$C^* \left(\equiv V(w_1, w_2, y) \right) \equiv w_1 x_1^* (w_1, w_2, y) + w_2 x_2^* (w_1, w_2, y).$$

This function, which shall henceforth be denoted by $C^*(w_1, w_2, y)$ is the firm's indirect cost function and is typically referred to simply as the *cost function*. It tells us the minimum cost associated with producing the output level y. It is the level of cost associated with the isocost line that passes through (x_1^*, x_2^*) in Figure 5.5. We shall now investigate the comparative statics properties of the model.

First, observe that by the Envelope Theorem,

$$C_y^*(w_1, w_2, y) = L_y = \lambda = \lambda^*(w_1, w_2, y).$$

Hence the multiplier measures the marginal cost of output, which we typically denote by MC. Again applying the Envelope Theorem, we observe that

$$C_{w_1}^*(w_1, w_2, y) = L_{w_1} = x_1 = x_1^*(w_1, w_2, y)$$

and

$$C_{w_2}^*(w_1, w_2, y) = L_{w_2} = x_2 = x_2^*(w_1, w_2, y).$$

This tells us that the partial derivative of the cost function with respect to any input price is the firm's conditional demand for that input. This result is known as *Shephard's Lemma*.

Now apply Young's Theorem to the cost function: Since

$$C_{w_1 w_2}^* = C_{w_2 w_1}^*$$

we have

$$\frac{\partial x_1^*}{\partial w_2} = \frac{\partial x_2^*}{\partial w_1}$$

our first reciprocity result. Explicit computation reveals these derivatives to be positive. In addition, since

$$C_{y w_1}^* = C_{w_1 y}^*$$

and

$$C^*_{yw_2} = C^*_{w_2 y}$$

we have the additional reciprocity results

$$\frac{\partial \lambda^*}{\partial w_1} = \frac{\partial x_1^*}{\partial y}$$

and

$$\frac{\partial \lambda^*}{\partial w_2} = \frac{\partial x_2^*}{\partial y}.$$

These rather non-intuitive results have some very interesting implications. As explicit computation reveals, the minimization hypothesis alone does not lead to a definitive sign prediction for these derivatives. If $\partial x_1^*/\partial y < 0$, we say that input one is *inferior*. The preceding result tells us that if w_1 increases and input one is inferior, then the MC curve must shift down. If $\partial x_1^*/\partial y > 0$, then input one is *normal* and an increase in w_1 will shift the MC curve upward.

Next we consider the conjugate pairs results. In this case, the theorem implies

$$L_{1w_1} \cdot \frac{\partial x_1^*}{\partial w_1} < 0 \quad \text{and} \quad L_{2w_2} \cdot \frac{\partial x_2^*}{\partial w_2} < 0.$$

Since $L_{1w_1} > 0$ and $L_{2w_2} > 0$, we observe that the conditional demand for each input is necessarily a decreasing function of its own price.

Finally, we consider the effect of a change in output on MC. Computation reveals that

$$\frac{\partial \lambda^*}{\partial y} = \frac{\begin{vmatrix} -\lambda^* f_{11} & -\lambda^* f_{12} & 0 \\ -\lambda^* f_{21} & -\lambda^* f_{22} & 0 \\ -f_1 & -f_2 & -1 \end{vmatrix}}{|H|} = \frac{-\lambda^* \left(f_{11} f_{22} - f_{12} f_{21} \right)}{|H|}.$$

Since $\lambda^* = \text{MC}$, this expression is MC_y. We know that $|H| < 0$ by the second-order condition. Furthermore, from the first-order conditions, we know that

$$\lambda^* = \frac{w_1}{f_1} = \frac{w_2}{f_2} > 0$$

since marginal productivities are positive. However, the sign of $f_{11}f_{22} - f_{12}f_{21}$ is indeterminant. Hence, without additional information, we cannot assert *on the basis of the minimization hypothesis alone* whether MC rises, falls, or remains constant as output increases. However, more can be said. We have assumed that this firm is a cost minimizing firm. Suppose that we adopt the stronger assumption that this firm is maximizing profit. Then, employing the fact that we stated just prior to this application, we may then assert that $f_{11}f_{22} - f_{12}f_{21} > 0$ *must* hold and therefore, MC is a (locally) increasing function of output. Thus, imposing additional structure on the model (based perhaps on other empirical information) has allowed us to obtain additional results.

5.6. Profit Maximization and the Le Châtelier Principle

Consider a profit maximizing firm that produces output y from inputs x_1 and x_2 with C^2 production $y = f(x_1, x_2)$. With output price p and input prices w_1 and w_2, profit is

$$\pi(x_1, x_2) = pf(x_1, x_2) - w_1 x_1 - w_2 x_2.$$

The first-order necessary conditions for a profit maximum are

$$\pi_1 = pf_1(x_1, x_2) - w_1 = 0$$

$$\pi_2 = pf_2(x_1, x_2) - w_2 = 0.$$

Now form the Hessian matrix

$$H = \begin{bmatrix} \pi_{11} & \pi_{12} \\ \pi_{21} & \pi_{22} \end{bmatrix} = \begin{bmatrix} pf_{11} & pf_{12} \\ pf_{21} & pf_{22} \end{bmatrix}.$$

The second-order sufficient conditions require that $pf_{11} < 0$ and $|H| > 0$ at the point where the first-order conditions hold. We assume the second-order conditions hold. The solution defines the profit maximizing input levels as differentiable functions of the parameters:

$$x_1 = x_1^*(p, w_1, w_2), \quad x_2 = x_2^*(p, w_1, w_2). \tag{2}$$

Substituting these solutions into the first-order conditions and differentiating with respect to w_1 yields the comparative statics derivative

$$\frac{\partial x_1^*}{\partial w_1} = \frac{f_{22}}{p(f_{11}f_{22} - f_{12}f_{21})} < 0 \tag{3}$$

(Note: $f_{22} < 0$ since the second-order conditions require $pf_{11} < 0$ and $p^2(f_{11}f_{22} - f_{12}f_{21}) > 0$. Since $f_{12} = f_{21}$, we must have $f_{11}f_{22} > (f_{12})^2 > 0$, implying that sign f_{22} = sign f_{11}.) A situation where both inputs are variable is typically referred to as a long-run situation. Hence, the input demand functions given by (2) and the comparative statics derivative given by (3) may be thought of as pertaining to a long-run situation since both inputs were variable. We shall denote the derivative in (3) by

$$\left(\frac{\partial x_1^*}{\partial w_1} \right)_0$$

since there were zero fixed inputs in the profit maximization problem.

In contrast, a situation where some input level is fixed is called a short-run situation. Suppose now that the firm is operating at the long-run optimum (x_1^*, x_2^*). Furthermore, suppose that input two becomes *fixed* at $x_2 = x_2^*$. Obviously, $x_1 = x_1^*$ remains optimal; but the firm is now in a short-run situation and *the comparative statics properties of the model have been altered.*

Since the firm may now optimize with respect to x_1 only, the first-order necessary condition for a profit maximum is simply

$$\pi_1 = pf_1(x_1, x_2^*) - w_1 = 0 \tag{4}$$

and $pf_{11} < 0$ is the second-order condition that is satisfied as a result of the second-order conditions for the original long-run problem. Now (4) defines the solution as a differentiable function of the parameters:

$$x_1 = x_1^*(p, w_1, x_2^*).$$

(Note that x_2^* is a parameter here since it enters (4) as a constant.) Substituting this solution into (4) and differentiating with respect to w_1 yields

$$\frac{\partial x_1^*}{\partial w_1} = \frac{1}{pf_{11}} < 0. \tag{5}$$

Since there was one fixed input here, we shall denote this derivative by

$$\left(\frac{\partial x_1^*}{\partial w_1}\right)_1.$$

Claim:

$$\left(\frac{\partial x_1^*}{\partial w_1}\right)_0 \leq \left(\frac{\partial x_1^*}{\partial w_1}\right)_1.$$

Proof: Since $f_{12} = f_{21}$, $-f_{12}f_{21} = -(f_{12})^2 \leq 0$. Now, add $f_{11}f_{22}$ to both sides of the inequality:

$$f_{11}f_{22} - f_{12}f_{21} \leq f_{11}f_{22}.$$

Multiplying by $p > 0$ yields

$$p(f_{11}f_{22} - f_{12}f_{21}) \leq pf_{11}f_{22}.$$

Since the term in parentheses is positive by the second-order condition,

$$1 \le \frac{pf_{11}f_{22}}{p(f_{11}f_{22} - f_{12}f_{21})}.$$

Now, divide both sides by $pf_{11} < 0$ to obtain

$$\left(\frac{\partial x_1}{\partial w_1}\right)_1 = \frac{1}{pf_{11}} \ge \frac{f_{22}}{p(f_{11}f_{22} - f_{12}f_{21})} = \left(\frac{\partial x_1}{\partial w_1}\right)_0.$$

This result is known as the Le Châtelier Principle and may be interpreted as follows. Consider the long-run input demand functions given by (2). Let p and w_2 be fixed at $\bar{p}$ and $\bar{w}_2$, respectively. Then

$$x_1 = x_1^* (\bar{p}, w_1, \bar{w}_2) \text{ and } x_2 = x_2^*(\bar{p}, w_1, \bar{w}_2).$$

These formulas tell us how x_1^* and x_2^* adjust to changes in w_1 in the long-run, given that $(p, w_2) = (\bar{p}, \bar{w}_2)$. The relationship $x_1 = x_1^* (\bar{p}, w_1, \bar{w}_2)$ gives us the firm's long-run demand curve for input one, which is shown in Figure 5.6.

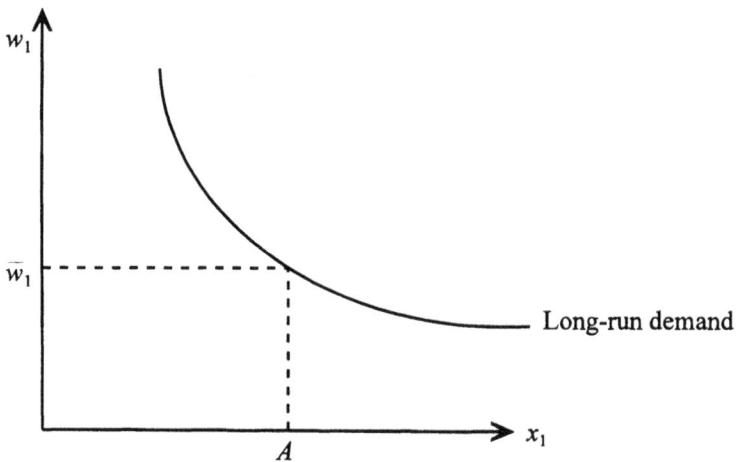

Figure 5.6

Now, suppose $w_1 = \bar{w}_1$. The long-run input demands are therefore $A \equiv x_1^*(\bar{p}, \bar{w}_1, \bar{w}_2)$ and $B \equiv x_2^*(\bar{p}, \bar{w}_1, \bar{w}_2)$. The slope of the long-run demand curve at this point is

$$\left(\frac{\partial x_1^*}{\partial w_1}\right)_0.$$

However, if x_2 is held fixed at $B(= x_2^*)$, the slope of the short-run demand curve at this point is

$$\left(\frac{\partial x_1^*}{\partial w_1}\right)_1 \geq \left(\frac{\partial x_1^*}{\partial w_1}\right)_0.$$

The long-run and short-run input demand curves passing through the point $(A, \bar{w}_1)$ appear as in Figure 5.7.

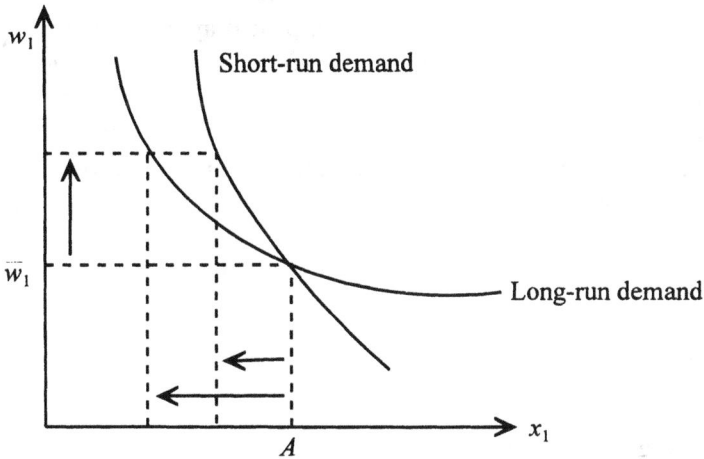

Figure 5.7

Recall that we are measuring x_1 on the horizontal axis. This fact, along with the demonstrated relationship between the long-run and short-run comparative statics derivatives imply that the short-run input demand must be steeper (i.e., less elastic) than its long-run counterpart. Observe also that if w_1 increases, the long-run reduction in the employment of the input is larger than the short-run reduction (unless $f_{12} = 0$, in which case the long-run and short-run response are the same, as can be seen using (3) and (5)).

5.7 Two Approaches to Comparative Statics Analysis

We have seen in this chapter that there are two equivalent approaches to studying the comparative statics properties of optimization-based models. The first approach is called the *primal* approach and involves explicitly solving the optimization problem and directly computing the comparative statics derivatives. This was the approach taken in Chapter 4. Alternatively, one may exploit the properties of the value function (indirect objective function). This is called the *dual* approach.

Given the extensive computation rendered necessary by the primal approach, duality theory is quite convenient. Its empirical application generally involves specification of a functional form for an *indirect* objective function. One must be mindful of the fact that this indirect objective function must satisfy certain properties that are direct consequences of the optimization hypothesis. For example, we saw in Application 5.3 that the (indirect) cost function C^* satisfies the symmetry property

$$C^*_{w_1 w_2} = C^*_{w_2 w_1},$$

which implied

$$\frac{\partial x_1^*}{\partial w_2} = \frac{\partial x_2^*}{\partial w_1}.$$

Thus, *if cost minimization is assumed*, this symmetry must be *imposed* when attempting to obtain econometric estimates of the conditional input demands.

Note: The Le Châtelier Principle takes its name from the tendency of thermodynamic systems to exhibit the same type of behavior. Again, this result is a direct consequence of the maximization hypothesis.

Problems

1. A consumer maximizes the quasilinear utility function $u(x) + y$ subject to the budget constraint $px + y = M$, where $u' > 0$, $u'' < 0$, and the price of good y is assumed to be one.

   a. Show that the demand for x is independent of M.

   b. Denote the demand for x by $x^*(p)$. Show that

   $$\frac{dx^*}{dp} < 0.$$

   c. Determine $y^*(p, M)$.

   d. Let $V(p, M)$ denote the value function (Note: in this context, V is called the *indirect utility function*.) Use the Envelope Theorem to show that

   $$V_p(p, M) = -x^*.$$

   (This result is known as *Roy's Identity*.)

   e. Show that $V_M(p, M)$ is constant. How do you interpret this?

2. A firm produces output y and has cost function $c(y)$, which satisfies $c' > 0$ and $c'' > 0$. Output price is p. Some of the output of the firm is defective and hence cannot be sold. Specifically, the probability that any one unit of output is *not defective* is q, $0 < q < 1$. The firm's expected profit is therefore

   $$E[\pi] = pqy - c(y).$$

   a. Let y^* maximize $E[\pi]$. Compute

   $$\frac{dy^*}{dq}$$

   and determine its sign.

b. Let $E^*[\pi]$ denote the value function (i.e., the indirect expected profit function). Use the Envelope Theorem to show that

$$\frac{dE^*[\pi]}{dq} > 0.$$

c. Now compute this derivative directly, without appealing to the Envelope Theorem.

3. The tire manufacturer in Application 3.4 has cost function

$$C(x_1, x_2) = 3x_1^2 - 2x_1x_2 + x_2^2$$

and must satisfy $x_1 + x_2 = T$.

a. Compute the value function $C^*(T)$. Compute

$$\frac{dC^*}{dT} \left(= MC^* \right)$$

and explain what this derivative measures.

b. Suppose now that $T = 6$. Using the results from Application 3.4, we know that $x_1^* = 2$ and $x_2^* = 4$. Suppose x_2 is now *fixed* at 4 and that the firm must continue to fulfill the contract. Determine the solution value of x_1 and denote it by $\tilde{x}_1$.

c. With no constraint, we know that

$$x_1^* = \frac{T}{3}.$$

With x_2 fixed at 4, we have $\tilde{x}_1 = T - 4$. Graph x_1^* and $\tilde{x}_1$ as functions of T. Where do these lines intersect? Which rises most rapidly?

d. Compute the (constrained) value function

$$\tilde{C}(\tilde{x}_1, 4)$$

and

$$\frac{d\tilde{C}}{dT} \left(= \tilde{MC} \right).$$

e. Graph MC^* and $\tilde{MC}$. Where do they intersect? Which rises most rapidly?

4. A multiproduct firm produces outputs y_1 and y_2 from a single input x with production function

$$x = f(y_1, y_2).$$

Output prices are p_1 and p_2. The firm has a fixed amount $\bar{x}$ of the input available and maximizes sales revenue subject to its production function.

a. Let $L = p_1 y_1 + p_2 y_2 + \lambda(\bar{x} - f(y_1, y_2))$ denote the Lagrangian for the firm's constrained revenue maximization problem. Let

$$y_1 = y_1^*(p_1, p_2, \bar{x}), y_2 = y_2^*(p_1, p_2 \bar{x}), \lambda = \lambda^*(p_1, p_2, \bar{x})$$

denote the solution. How do you interpret λ^*?

b. Let R^* = the value function (i.e., the indirect revenue function). Show that

$$R_{p_1}^* = y_1^* \quad \text{and} \quad R_{p_2}^* = y_2^*,$$

which is a revenue counterpart to Shephard's Lemma.

c. Use Theorems 5-1B and 5-3B to state reciprocity and conjugate pair results for y_1^*, y_2^* and λ^*. Confirm your results by direct computation.

d. Illustrate graphically showing the production constraint and several isorevenue lines in (y_1, y_2) space.

5. Consider a firm producing two outputs y_1 and y_2 from input x according to the production function

$$x = g(y_1, y_2).$$

Output prices are p_1 and p_2, and the input price is w. The firm maximizes profit

$$\pi = p_1 y_1 + p_2 y_2 - wg(y_1, y_2).$$

Let $\pi^* (p_1, p_2, w)$ denote the value (indirect profit) function. Show that

(i) $\dfrac{\partial y_1^*}{\partial p_1} > 0, \quad \dfrac{\partial y_2^*}{\partial p_2} > 0, \quad \dfrac{\partial x^*}{\partial w} < 0$

(ii) $\pi^*_{p_1} = y_1^*, \quad \pi^*_{p_2} = y_2^*, \quad \pi^*_w = -x^*$

(iii) $\dfrac{\partial y_1^*}{\partial p_2} = \dfrac{\partial y_2^*}{\partial p_1} \qquad \dfrac{\partial y_1^*}{\partial w} = \dfrac{-\partial x^*}{\partial p_1}$

$\dfrac{\partial y_2^*}{\partial w} = \dfrac{-\partial x^*}{\partial p_2}$

6. Suppose that a firm produces output y from input x according to the production function

$$y = ln(x).$$

Output price is p and the input price is w. Let x^* denote the profit maximizing input level and y^* the corresponding output level.

a. Verify the formulas derived in Application 5.2 for this technology.
b. Compute the value (indirect profit) function π^*.
c. Verify the conjugate pair, envelope, and reciprocity results for this technology.

7. A firm with production function $y = x_1 x_2$ solves the cost minimization problem

    Minimize $w_1 x_1 + w_2 x_2$ subject to $y = x_1 x_2$.

    Let C^* denote the value (cost) function.

    a. Verify Shephard's Lemma.
    b. State reciprocity and conjugate pair results for the cost minimization problem. Are the input demand curves downward sloping? Verify your claims via direct computation.

6. Introduction to Primal-Dual Analysis

In this chapter, we discuss an alternative comparative statics methodology called *primal-dual analysis*. Primal-dual analysis is a powerful, computationally efficient method for performing comparative statics analysis. Conditions on various (bordered) Hessian determinants will be seen to impose restrictions on the size and sign of comparative statics derivatives. Moreover, these restrictions constitute all known comparative statics implications of the optimization hypothesis. Primal-dual analysis is therefore a unifying method that allows us to discover all implied restrictions on observable phenomena.

We begin with a discussion of the concept of (border-preserving) principal minors of a square matrix.

6.1. (Border-Preserving) Principal Minors

Consider the square (3×3) matrix

$$A = \begin{bmatrix} a_{11} & a_{12} & a_{13} \\ a_{21} & a_{22} & a_{23} \\ a_{31} & a_{32} & a_{33} \end{bmatrix}.$$

A *principal minor* of A is the determinant of the matrix that remains when any $3 - k$ rows and corresponding columns are deleted. Any principal minor of order k is the determinant of a $k \times k$ matrix. For example, deleting row 3 and column 3 from A yields the second-order principal minor

$$\begin{vmatrix} a_{11} & a_{12} \\ a_{21} & a_{22} \end{vmatrix}.$$

If we delete row 2 and column 2 as well as row 3 and column 3 from A, we obtain the first-order principal minor

$$\begin{vmatrix} a_{11} \end{vmatrix}.$$

For A, there are obviously three second-order and three first-order principal minors.

Now consider the 4×4 matrix

$$B = \begin{bmatrix} a_{11} & a_{12} & a_{13} & b_1 \\ a_{21} & a_{22} & a_{23} & b_2 \\ a_{31} & a_{32} & a_{33} & b_3 \\ b_1 & b_2 & b_3 & 0 \end{bmatrix}.$$

Note how the bs *border* the as, which constitute a 3×3 submatrix. A *border-preserving principal minor* of M is the determinant of the matrix that remains when any $3 - k$ rows and corresponding columns are deleted, *provided that the border is not deleted*. Since the border may not be deleted in this construction, any border-preserving principal minor of order k is the determinant of a $(k + 1) \times (k + 1)$ matrix. For example, when $k = 1$, we delete $3 - 1 = 2$ rows and corresponding columns obtaining a 2×2 determinant. Deleting, for instance, row 1 and column 1 as well as row 2 and column 2 yields a border-preserving principal minor of order one, given by

$$\begin{vmatrix} a_{33} & b_3 \\ b_3 & 0 \end{vmatrix}.$$

When $k = 2$, we delete any $3 - 2 = 1$ row and corresponding column, obtaining a 3×3 determinant. Deleting, for instance, row 1 and column 1 yields a border-preserving principal minor of order two, given by

$$\begin{vmatrix} a_{22} & a_{23} & b_2 \\ a_{32} & a_{33} & b_3 \\ b_2 & b_3 & 0 \end{vmatrix}.$$

6.2. Comparative Statics with Unconstrained Optimization Using Primal-Dual Analysis

Consider the problem

Maximize $F(x, a)$
   x

where F is C^2 and a is a parameter. Let $x = x^*(a)$ denote the solution where the second-order sufficient condition $F_{xx} < 0$ is assumed to hold. Let $V(a) \equiv F(x^*(a), a)$ denote the corresponding value function. Consider now a new function given by

$$G(x, a) = F(x, a) - V(a).$$

The function $G(x, a)$ is called the *primal-dual objective function* and tells us the difference between the actual value of F and the maximum value of F for any a. Now by definition, $V(a)$ is the maximum value of $F(x, a)$, hence

$$F(x, a) \leq V(a)$$

for all $x \neq x^*$ and $F(x, a) = V(a)$ when $x = x^*$. Therefore G has a maximum (of zero) when $x = x^*$. This is illustrated in Figure 6.1.

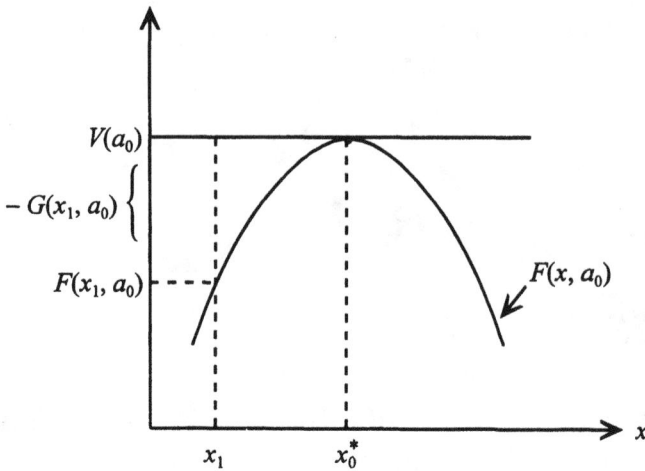

Figure 6.1

Suppose $a = a_0$ and let $F(x, a_0)$ denote the objective function when a is fixed at this value. Let x_0^* denote the point where $F(x, a_0)$ is maximum. $V(a_0)$ is the maximum value of $F(x, a_0)$. Now, let x_1 be any other point. G is simply the difference between $F(x_1, a_0)$ and $V(a_0)$, the negative of the distance between $V(a_0)$ and $F(x_1, a_0)$ on the vertical axis. Observe that $G = 0$ precisely when $x = x_0^*$, hence $G(x_0^*, a_0^*) = 0$. thus we may assert

(i) when $a = a_0$, $x = x_0^*$ is optimal.

Now consider Figure 6.2.

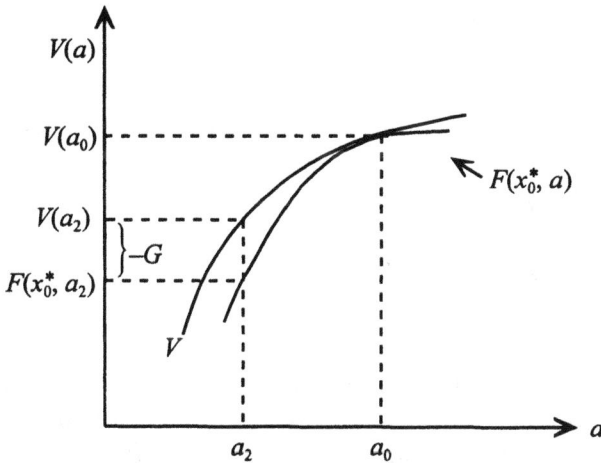

Figure 6.2

The curve labeled V is the graph of the value function. We know that when $a = a_0$, $V = V(a_0)$. We also know that with x fixed at x_0^*, $F(x_0^*, a) \leq V(a)$ with equality when $a = a_0$. Hence the graph of $F(x_0^*, a)$ appears as shown. Since the graph of $F(x_0^*, a)$ is tangent to V at a_0, their slopes are equal, which implies

$$F_a(x_0^*, a_0) = V'(a_0),$$

which is the Envelope result proven in Section 5.1.

Now let a_2 be any other point. G is simply the difference between $F(x_0^*, a_2)$ and $V(a_2)$. Observe that $G = 0$ precisely when $a = a_0$. Hence $G(x_0^*, a_0) = 0$ as asserted before. Therefore

(ii) when $x = x_0^*$, $a = a_0$ is optimal.

The implication of the preceding discussion is that the maximum position of $G(x, a)$ may be described by the usual first- and second-order conditions, where x *and* a are both treated as *variables* in the optimization. Hence, the first-order necessary conditions for a maximum of $G(x, a)$ are

$$G_x(x, a) = F_x(x, a) = 0 \tag{1}$$

$$G_a(x, a) = F_a(x, a) - V'(a) = 0. \tag{2}$$

Now, form the Hessian matrix

$$H = \begin{bmatrix} G_{xx} & G_{xa} \\ G_{ax} & G_{aa} \end{bmatrix} = \begin{bmatrix} F_{xx} & F_{xa} \\ F_{ax} & F_{aa} - V'' \end{bmatrix}.$$

Assuming that the second-order sufficient conditions for a maximum of G hold, we have $F_{xx} < 0$ and, since $|H|$ must be positive, $F_{aa} - V'' < 0$. *This inequality (or its higher dimensional counterpart) is the fundamental inequality from which all comparative statics results are obtained.* Note that in the first-order condition, (1) is the usual result for the primal problem. More important, however, is the fact that (2) is the Envelope Theorem proven in Section 5.1.

To see how to use the inequality $F_{aa} - V'' < 0$, let $x = x^*(a)$ denote the solution to the problem and substitute into (2), yielding the identity

$$F_a(x^*(a), a) - V'(a) \equiv 0.$$

Differentiation with respect to a yields

$$F_{ax} \cdot \frac{dx^*}{da} + F_{aa} - V''(a) = 0.$$

Since $F_{aa} - V'' < 0$, we conclude that

$$F_{ax} \cdot \frac{dx^*}{da} > 0$$

or sign F_{ax} = sign F_{xa} = sign dx^*/da, which is the Conjugate Pairs Theorem proven in Section 5.1.

Now, consider

Maximize $F(x, y, a, b, c)$
  x, y

where F is C^2. Let $V(a, b, c)$ denote the value function. The primal-dual problem is

$$\text{Maximize} \quad F(x, y, a, b, c) - V(a, b, c).$$
$$x, y, a, b, c$$

The first-order necessary conditions are

$$F_x = 0 \quad \text{and} \quad F_y = 0$$

as well as

$$F_a - V_a = 0, \quad F_b - V_b = 0, \quad \text{and } F_c - V_c = 0.$$

The first two equalities are the first-order conditions for the primal problem. The last three equalities are the Envelope results for the problem that we proved in Theorem 5-2A for the case of two parameters.

In the previous problem, we had among the second-order conditions $F_{aa} - V'' < 0$. Here, its counterpart is the following. Consider the matrix

$$M = \begin{bmatrix} F_{aa} - V_{aa} & F_{ab} - V_{ab} & F_{ac} - V_{ac} \\ F_{ba} - V_{ba} & F_{bb} - V_{bb} & F_{bc} - V_{bc} \\ F_{ca} - V_{ca} & F_{cb} - V_{cb} & F_{cc} - V_{cc} \end{bmatrix}.$$

What is required is that every principal minor of *odd* order be ≤ 0 and every principal minor of *even* order be ≥ 0. This implies in particular that the diagonal elements of the above matrix are all nonpositive (since they are the three principal minors of order 1). When this is the case, we say that *M is negative semidefinite*. All comparative statics results for this problem derive from these inequalities.

Application 6.1

In Section 5.6, we considered the profit maximization problem

$$\underset{x_1,\, x_2}{\text{Maximize}}\ pf(x_1, x_2) - w_1 x_1 - w_2 x_2$$

We shall investigate the comparative statics properties of this model via the primal-dual methodology.

Let $\pi^*(p, w_1, w_2)$ denote the value (indirect profit) function. The primal-dual problem is

$$\underset{x_1,\, x_2,\, p,\, w_1,\, w_2}{\text{Maximize}}\ G(x_1, x_2, p, w_1, w_2) = pf(x_1, x_2) - w_1 x_1 - w_2 x_2 - \pi^*(p, w_1, w_2)$$

The first-order necessary conditions are

$$G_1 = pf_1(x_1, x_2) - w_1 = 0 \tag{3}$$

$$G_2 = pf_2(x_1, x_2) - w_2 = 0 \tag{4}$$

$$G_p = y - \pi_p^*(p, w_1, w_2) = 0 \tag{5}$$

$$G_{w_1} = -x_1 - \pi_{w_1}^*(p, w_1, w_2) = 0 \tag{6}$$

$$G_{w_2} = -x_2 - \pi_{w_2}^*(p, w_1, w_2) = 0 \tag{7}$$

Observe that (3) and (4) are the usual (primal) profit maximization conditions. Let (x_1^*, x_2^*) solve (3) and (4) and let $y^* = f(x_1^*, x_2^*)$. Then (5), (6), and (7) yield

$$y^* = \pi_p^*(p, w_1, w_2)$$

$$-x_1^* = \pi_{w_1}^*(p, w_1, w_2)$$

and

$$-x_2^* = \pi_{w_2}^*(p, w_1, w_2),$$

which is Hotelling's Lemma for the two-input firm.

Now, as stated previously, the second-order conditions for a maximum of the primal-dual problem *include* that the matrix

$$H = \begin{bmatrix} G_{pp} & G_{pw_1} & G_{pw_2} \\ G_{w_1 p} & G_{w_1 w_1} & G_{w_1 w_2} \\ G_{w_2 p} & G_{w_2 w_1} & G_{w_2 w_2} \end{bmatrix}$$

be negative semidefinite at the point where (3) – (7) hold. Using (5) – (7), we have

$$G_{pp} = -\pi_{pp}^* \qquad G_{pw_1} = -\pi_{pw_1}^* \qquad G_{pw_2} = -\pi_{pw_2}^*$$

$$G_{w_1 p} = -\pi_{w_1 p}^* \qquad G_{w_1 w_1} = -\pi_{w_1 w_1}^* \qquad G_{w_1 w_2} = -\pi_{w_1 w_2}^*$$

$$G_{w_2 p} = -\pi_{w_2 p}^* \qquad G_{w_2 w_1} = -\pi_{w_2 w_1}^* \qquad G_{w_2 w_2} = -\pi_{w_2 w_2}^*$$

Since $-x_1^* = \pi_{w_1}^*$ and $-x_2^* = \pi_{w_2}^*$, we have

$$-\pi_{w_1 p}^* = \frac{\partial x_1^*}{\partial p}, \qquad -\pi_{w_1 w_1}^* = \frac{\partial x_1^*}{\partial w_1}, \qquad -\pi_{w_1 w_2}^* = \frac{\partial x_1^*}{\partial w_2}$$

$$-\pi_{w_2 p}^* = \frac{\partial x_2^*}{\partial p}, \qquad -\pi_{w_2 w_1}^* = \frac{\partial x_2^*}{\partial w_1}, \qquad -\pi_{w_2 w_2}^* = \frac{\partial x_2^*}{\partial w_2}$$

In addition, since $y^* = \pi_p^*$, we have

$$-\pi^*_{pp} = -\frac{\partial y^*}{\partial p}, \quad -\pi^*_{pw_1} = -\frac{\partial y^*}{\partial w_1}, \quad -\pi^*_{pw_2} = -\frac{\partial y^*}{\partial w_2}$$

Therefore,

$$H = \begin{bmatrix} \dfrac{-\partial y^*}{\partial p} & \dfrac{-\partial y^*}{\partial w_1} & \dfrac{-\partial y^*}{\partial w_2} \\[3mm] \dfrac{\partial x_1^*}{\partial p} & \dfrac{\partial x_1^*}{\partial w_1} & \dfrac{\partial x_1^*}{\partial w_2} \\[3mm] \dfrac{\partial x_2^*}{\partial p} & \dfrac{\partial x_2^*}{\partial w_1} & \dfrac{\partial x_2^*}{\partial w_2} \end{bmatrix}$$

Since H must be negative semidefinite, we know that all odd-ordered principal minors must be ≤ 0 and all even-ordered principal minors must be ≥ 0. Since the diagonal elements are themselves principal minors of order one, we observe that

$$\frac{-\partial y^*}{\partial p} \leq 0, \quad \frac{\partial x_1^*}{\partial w_1} \leq 0 \quad \text{and} \quad \frac{\partial x_2^*}{\partial w_2} \leq 0,$$

i.e., the firm's output supply curve is not downward sloping and the input demand curves are not upward sloping. (In fact, assuming that the second-order sufficient conditions for profit maximization are satisfied, the above inequalities are strict. Hence, the input demand curves are downward sloping and the output supply curve is upward sloping.)

Returning now to the principal minors of H, delete row 3 and column 3 to obtain the second-order principal minor.

$$\begin{vmatrix} \dfrac{-\partial y^*}{\partial p} & \dfrac{-\partial y^*}{\partial w_1} \\[3mm] \dfrac{\partial x_1^*}{\partial p} & \dfrac{\partial x_1^*}{\partial w_1} \end{vmatrix}$$

This must have sign ≥ 0, hence

$$\left(\frac{-\partial y^*}{\partial p}\right)\left(\frac{\partial x_1^*}{\partial w_1}\right) \geq \left(\frac{-\partial y^*}{\partial w_1}\right)\left(\frac{\partial x_1^*}{\partial p}\right),$$

which says that the "own effects" outweigh the "cross effects." Deleting row 2 and column 2 likewise yields

$$\left(\frac{-\partial y^*}{\partial p}\right)\left(\frac{\partial x_2^*}{\partial w_2}\right) \geq \left(\frac{-\partial y^*}{\partial w_2}\right)\left(\frac{\partial x_2^*}{\partial p}\right).$$

Deleting row 1 and column 1 yields

$$\left(\frac{\partial x_1^*}{\partial w_1}\right)\left(\frac{\partial x_2^*}{\partial w_2}\right) \geq \left(\frac{\partial x_1^*}{\partial w_2}\right)\left(\frac{\partial x_2^*}{\partial w_1}\right),$$

which, again, actually holds strictly because of the second-order sufficient conditions for a profit maximum.

Finally, by Young's Theorem, H is symmetric; hence

$$\frac{-\partial y^*}{\partial w_1} = \frac{\partial x_1^*}{\partial p}, \quad \frac{-\partial y^*}{\partial w_2} = \frac{\partial x_2^*}{\partial p}$$

and

$$\frac{\partial x_1^*}{\partial w_2} = \frac{\partial x_2^*}{\partial w_1},$$

which are the reciprocity conditions.

6.3.   Comparative Statics with Constrained Optimization Using Primal-Dual Analysis

Consider the constrained maximization problem

Maximize $f(x, y, a, b, c)$ subject to $g(x, y, a, b, c) = 0$
x, y

where f and g are C^2. Let $L = f + \lambda g$ denote the Lagrangian function and denote the solution by $(x, y, \lambda) = (x^*, y^*, \lambda^*)$. The value function is denoted by $V(a, b, c)$.
    The primal-dual formulation for this constrained maximization problem is:

Maximize $f(x, y, a, b, c) - V(a, b, c)$ subject to $g(x, y, a, b, c) = 0$.
x, y, a, b, c

Let $L^* (x, y, a, b, c) = f(x, y, a, b, c) - V(a, b, c) + \lambda g(x, y, a, b, c)$. The first-order necessary conditions for a constrained maximum are

$$L^*_x = f_x + \lambda g_x = 0 \tag{6}$$

$$L^*_y = f_y + \lambda g_y = 0 \tag{7}$$

$$L^*_a = f_a - V_a + \lambda g_a = 0 \tag{8}$$

$$L^*_b = f_b - V_b + \lambda g_b = 0 \tag{9}$$

$$L^*_c = f_c - V_c + \lambda g_c = 0 \tag{10}$$

$$L^*_\lambda = g(x, y, a, b, c) = 0. \tag{11}$$

Now (6), (7), and (11) are the first-order conditions for the primal problem. Equations (8), (9), and (10) are the Envelope Theorem for the constrained problem (proven in Theorem 5-2B for the case of two parameters).
    Now let

$$H = \begin{bmatrix} L_{aa}^* & L_{ab}^* & L_{ac}^* & g_a \\ L_{ba}^* & L_{bb}^* & L_{bc}^* & g_b \\ L_{ca}^* & L_{cb}^* & L_{cc}^* & g_c \\ g_a & g_b & g_c & 0 \end{bmatrix}.$$

The second-order conditions now *include* the requirement that the border preserving principal minors of H of odd order be ≤ 0 and those of even order be ≥ 0. As in the unconstrained case, these determinental conditions yield all implications of the maximization hypothesis.

Application 6.2

Suppose that there are two industries in an economy that produce outputs q_1 and q_2 from the single input x according to the C^2 production functions

$$q_1 = q_1(x_1)$$

and

$$q_2 = q_2(x_2)$$

where x_1 denotes the amount of the x-input used by industry one and x_2 denotes the amount used by industry two. There is a total of x units of input to be allocated between the industries: $x_1 + x_2 = x$. The market prices of the outputs are p_1 and p_2. The objective of the economy is to maximize "national product" $NP = p_1 q_1 + p_2 q_2$ subject to the resource constraint:

Maximize $p_1 q_1(x_1) + p_2 q_2(x_2)$ subject to $x_1 + x_2 = x$
x_1, x_2

Note that the parameters here are p_1, p_2, and x. Let $NP^*(p_1, p_2, x)$ denote the value (indirect national product) function and assume that the second-order sufficient conditions hold for the primal problem.

The primal-dual problem is

$$\underset{x_1, x_2, p_1, p_2, x}{\text{Maximize}} \quad p_1 q_1(x_1) + p_2 q_2(x_2) - NP^*(p_1, p_2, x) + \lambda(x - x_1 - x_2).$$

As in Application 6.1, the first-order necessary conditions include the ones for the primal problem as well as

$$q_1 - NP^*_{p_1} = 0$$

$$q_2 - NP^*_{p_2} = 0$$

$$-NP^*_x + \lambda = 0.$$

The second-order conditions require examination of

$$H = \begin{bmatrix} -NP^*_{p_1 p_1} & -NP^*_{p_1 p_2} & -NP^*_{p_1 x} & 0 \\ -NP^*_{p_2 p_1} & -NP^*_{p_2 p_2} & -NP^*_{p_2 x} & 0 \\ -NP^*_{x p_1} & -NP^*_{x p_2} & -NP^*_{xx} & 1 \\ 0 & 0 & 1 & 0 \end{bmatrix}.$$

Use * to denote the solution values of the variables. Then, using the first-order conditions (the Envelope results), we have

$$H = \begin{bmatrix} \dfrac{-\partial q_1^*}{\partial p_1} & \dfrac{-\partial q_1^*}{\partial p_2} & \dfrac{-\partial q_1^*}{\partial x} & 0 \\ \dfrac{-\partial q_2^*}{\partial p_1} & \dfrac{-\partial q_2^*}{\partial p_2} & \dfrac{-\partial q_2^*}{\partial x} & 0 \\ \dfrac{-\partial \lambda^*}{\partial p_1} & \dfrac{-\partial \lambda^*}{\partial p_2} & \dfrac{-\partial \lambda^*}{\partial x} & 1 \\ 0 & 0 & 1 & 0 \end{bmatrix}.$$

The reciprocity results are therefore

$$\frac{\partial q_1^*}{\partial p_2} = \frac{\partial q_2^*}{\partial p_1}, \quad \frac{\partial q_1^*}{\partial x} = \frac{\partial \lambda^*}{\partial p_1} \text{ and } \frac{\partial q_2^*}{\partial x} = \frac{\partial \lambda^*}{\partial p_2}.$$

Examination of border-preserving principal minors yields additional results. Deleting any *one* row and corresponding column yields a border-preserving principal minor of order 2, which must be ≥ 0. Deleting row 1 and column 1, one obtains

$$\frac{\partial q_2^*}{\partial p_2} \geq 0.$$

Similarly, deleting row 2 and column 2 implies

$$\frac{\partial q_1^*}{\partial p_1} \geq 0.$$

As if often the case, the solution value of the Lagrange multiplier and its comparative statics properties are of interest. In this model, λ^* is the rate of change of maximum *NP* with respect to changes in x, the total amount of the input available. When these industries are perfectly competitive, λ^* is the value of the marginal product of x, which is precisely what input x must be paid. Note, however, that unlike p_1 and p_2, λ^* is an *endogenously determined* shadow price (or "imputed value"). In other words, λ^* is determined as part of the solution of the model, unlike p_1 and p_2, which enter the model as parameters. However, the signs of the comparative statics derivatives

$$\frac{\partial \lambda^*}{\partial p_1}, \quad \frac{\partial \lambda^*}{\partial p_2} \text{ and } \frac{\partial \lambda^*}{\partial x}$$

are indeterminant *on the basis of the maximization hypothesis alone*. In Problem 6.4 you are asked to introduce additional assumptions that cause the signs of these comparative statics derivatives to become determinant.

Note: The primal-dual problem was introduced by Samuelson (1965) and fully developed by Silberberg (1974a, 1974b, 1978). For brevity, we have omitted proofs of some of the assertions made in this chapter regarding second-order conditions for the primal-dual problem. Consult Silberberg (1974a, 1974b) for details.

Problems

1. Use primal-dual analysis to obtain the results from Problem 5 in Chapter 5 for the profit function

    $$\pi = p_1 y_1 + p_2 y_2 - wg(y_1, y_2).$$

2. Use primal-dual analysis to derive the properties of the cost function obtained in Application 5.3.

3. Suppose that a consumer has the utility function $u(x, y)$ with budget constraint $px + y = M$. Let (x^*, y^*) denote the solution to the utility maximization problem. Show that the maximization hypothesis implies that the *substitution terms* satisfy

    $$x_p^* + x^* \cdot x_M^* \le 0$$

    and

    $$y_p^* + x^* \cdot y_M^* \ge 0.$$

4. In Application 6.2, no sign is implied for the comparative statics derivative

    $$\frac{\partial \lambda^*}{\partial x}$$

    on the basis of the maximization hypothesis alone.

    a. Explain what this derivative measures.
    b. What *additional assumptions* could be imposed on the problem that would make this derivative's sign determinant? How do you interpret these assumptions?

Answers to Selected Problems

Chapter 3

1. $P^* = \dfrac{M}{3}, \ x^* = \dfrac{2M}{3}$

4. $y^* = \dfrac{a - c - t}{2b}, \quad p^* = \dfrac{a + c + t}{2}$

6. $y_1^* = \dfrac{p_1}{2w}, \ y_2^* = \dfrac{p_2}{2w}, \ x^* = \dfrac{p_1^2 + p_2^2}{4w^2}$

Chapter 4

1. $\dfrac{dC^*}{dt} = \dfrac{-D'}{D' - S'} < 0, \quad \dfrac{dP^*}{dt} = \dfrac{-S'}{D' - S'} > 0$

3. $\dfrac{\partial x^*}{\partial n} = \dfrac{-B'}{nB''}, \quad \dfrac{\partial x^*}{\partial c} = \dfrac{1}{nB''}$

9. $\dfrac{dy^*}{dn} = \dfrac{y^*}{-n + D' \cdot MC'} < 0, \quad \dfrac{dY^*}{dn} = \dfrac{ny^*}{-n + D' \cdot MC'} + y^* > 0$

$\dfrac{dp^*}{dn} = MC' \cdot \dfrac{dy^*}{dn} < 0.$

Chapter 4 continued

10. $\dfrac{\partial p^*}{\partial w} = \dfrac{AC_w}{1 - AC_y \cdot D_p} > 0 \qquad \dfrac{\partial p^*}{\partial M} = \dfrac{AC_y \cdot D_M}{1 - AC_y \cdot D_p} < 0$

$\dfrac{\partial y^*}{\partial w} = D_p \cdot \dfrac{\partial p^*}{\partial w} < 0 \qquad \dfrac{\partial y^*}{\partial M} = \dfrac{D_M}{1 - AC_y \cdot D_p} > 0$

Chapter 5

3. $C^* = \dfrac{T^2}{3},\ MC^* = \dfrac{2T}{3},\ \tilde{x}_1 = T - 4,\ \widetilde{MC} = 6\left(T - 4\right) - 8$, intersection at $T = 6$

Chapter 6

4. $\lambda^* = \dfrac{\Delta NP^*}{\Delta x}$; $q_1'', q_2'' < 0$ (decreasing returns in each industry) implies

$\dfrac{\partial \lambda^*}{\partial x} < 0$

Selected References

Bartle, R.G., *The Elements of Real Analysis*, Second Edition. Wiley, 1976.

Beattie, B.R. and C.R. Taylor, *The Economics of Production*. Krieger, 1993

Chiang, A.C., *Fundamental Methods of Mathematical Economics*, Third Edition. McGraw-Hill, 1984.

Hands, D.W., *Introductory Mathematical Economics*. Heath, 1991.

Henderson, J.M. and R.E. Quandt, *Microeconomic Theory: A Mathematical Approach*, Third Edition. McGraw-Hill, 1980.

Hicks, J.R., *Value and Capital*. Oxford: Clarendon Press, 1946.

Klein, M.W., *Mathematical Methods for Economics*. Addison-Wesley, 1998.

Samuelson, P.A. *Foundations of Economic Analysis*. Cambridge, MA: Harvard University Press, 1947.

Samuelson, P.A., "Using Full Duality to Show that Simultaneously Additive Direct and Indirect Utilities Implies Unitary Price Elasticity of Demand," *Econometrica*, 33, 1965: 781–796.

Silberberg, E., "The Le Châtelier Principal as a Corollary to a Generalized Envelope Theorem," *Journal of Economic Theory*, 3, June 1971: 146–155.

Silberberg, E., "A Revision of Comparative Statics Methodology in Economics, or How to Do Comparative Statics on the Back of an Envelope," *Journal of Economic Theory*, 7, February 1974: 159–172.

Silberberg, E., "The Theory of the Firm in Long Run Equilibrium," *American Economic Review*, 64, September 1974: 734–741.

Silberberg, E., *The Structure of Economics: A Mathematical Analysis*, Second Edition. McGraw-Hill, 1978.

Simon, C.P. and L. Blume, *Mathematics for Economists*. Norton, 1994.

Stiglitz, J. (ed.), *The Collected Scientific Papers of Paul A. Samuelson*. Cambridge, MA: The M.I.T. Press, 1966.

Sydsaeter, K. and P.J. Hammond, *Mathematics for Economic Analysis*. Prentice-Hall, 1995.

Varian, H.F., *Microeconomic Analysis*, Third Edition. Norton, 1992.

Viner, J., "Cost Curves and Supply Curves," *Zeitschrift fur Nationalokonomie*, 3, 1931. Reprinted int *AEA Readings in Price Theory*. Homewood, IL: Irwin, 1952.

Index

www.ingramcontent.com/pod-product-compliance
Lightning Source LLC
Chambersburg PA
CBHW050643190326
41458CB00008B/2395